D1397988

Small food

Small food brigid kennedy

Photography by Louise Lister

SIMON & SCHUSTER
AUSTRALIA

To my son Benjamin – my best work

SMALL FOOD
First published in Australia in 2001 by
Simon & Schuster (Australia) Pty Limited
20 Barcoo Street, East Roseville NSW 2069

A Viacom Company
Sydney New York London Toronto Tokyo Singapore

© Brigid Kennedy 2001

All rights reseved. No part of this publication may be reproduced,
stored in a retrieval system, or transmitted, in any form or by any means,
electronic, mechanical, photocopying, recording or otherwise,
without the prior permission of the publisher in writing.

National Library of Australia
Cataloguing-in-Publication data

Kennedy, Brigid.
Small food.

Includes index.
ISBN 0 7318 1033 3.

1. Snack foods. 2. Appetizers. I. Title

641.812

Design & art direction: Yolande Gray Design
Photography: Louise Lister
Styling & food: Brigid Kennedy
Colour separations: Response, Sydney
Typeset in Din 9.5/13
Printed in China by Everbest Printing Company Ltd

10 9 8 7 6 5 4 3 2 1

Contents

One of the great pleasures in life is food; another is celebration. As a professional caterer (and eager party-goer!) I know only too well that people want to mark an occasion, as we love to single out those special things that happen in life.

The 1990s was a decade of burgeoning interest in all things edible and fun, and an ongoing obsession with lifestyle ensured that the shelves of magazine stores and bookstores now groan with food-related magazines and coffee-table books. Yet for some reason, hardcore party food has been an area largely ignored by our food writers and home-team chefs. That's where this book comes in.

Throughout **Small Food** you'll come across some familiar ingredients and combinations. While I have used a number of cocktail-food standbys for inspiration and borrowed from a spread of cuisines, my real joy has been in devising novel twists on classic and contemporary dishes. Ingredients and techniques once strangers to the world of hors d'oeuvres are here featured strongly.

It's my philosophy that simplicity of preparation and quality ingredients are paramount. The consumption of fresh, simply prepared food has never been more in vogue. While we strive to eat less and for health - less volume, less fat - we also want more variety in our diets. Today's guests crave new flavours and new combinations, and they're also more likely to indulge in something they'd normally consider 'wicked' if it's in a bite-sized portion.

The menus on these pages are designed to keep you in charge. The recipes are divided into handy, practical chapters entitled Occasions, Influences, and Seasons, with subsections devoted to specific themes. There's also a section called Master Recipes: easy to make, these are your launch-pad for making a huge array of party nibbles. And best of all, you can prepare them ahead of time.

Many people feel daunted by the prospect of planning a party and entertaining a room full of people. **Small Food** gives valuable hints on how to create the all-important mood for your party - that sense of occasion. With a little planning and preparation you'll avoid unnecessary stress, and by the time the doorbell chimes you'll be relaxed, happy in the knowledge that you're going to have just as good a time as your guests.

Party on!

Introduction

Staff

Whether you're a professional caterer or a home cook who loves to entertain, the rule is the same: always pay careful attention to who is going to be cleaning up! After you've organised a function, however big or small, having to clean up is the ultimate anticlimax. No matter what the style of party, and no matter what the budget, the clean-up person is always the one I organise first. It's horrible to have to clean up straight after a party or the next day, hangover or no hangover. After all, the person who creates the occasion should be able to enjoy the party, too. Even if you can't afford to pay a lot, there's usually someone about who's eager to earn a little extra cash – a student, say.

Of course, there are many styles of function and budget sizes. Let's start from the top end and work down.

staging a party
A party can't live by food alone ...

Large and formal

Professional caterers will generally provide their own cooks and waiters, who will be well versed in the sort of food they're serving. When shopping around for a caterer, get as many quotes as you can. Ask to see pictures of their product so you can decide if their style suits you. Many catering firms now post full details, including menus, prices and pictures of their food, on their own websites. For a full food-and-drinks service, you'll need to hire one waiter for every 20–25 guests.

If you can, hire your staff on the recommendation of a friend or colleague who's used them before and been satisfied. There are numerous agencies for waiters, but some are better than others. Personally, I prefer smaller, more personal agencies. An agency with a good reputation is likely to offer the best staff, and remember that cheapest doesn't mean best.

Large and casual

On these occasions, have the guests go to the bar for drinks. Certainly, it's more casual than having drinks served by waiters, but it keeps costs down and may allow you to spend a bit more on, say, the decorations. You'll need to allow for at least one of the food waiters to assist the bar-person in getting the first round of drinks out. Here, the rule of thumb is to hire one bar-person per 100 guests and one waiter per 50 guests.

For private parties, ask your caterer/waiters' agency if they offer a cash rate. This is a discount sometimes given if you pay your bill in cash, since credit card payments attract bank fees and lessen the supplier's profit. Some companies also offer discounts to regular customers who have accounts.

Staff should arrive up to an hour before the function commences, depending on their role. If there are several waiters/bar staff, stagger their starting times to make the most of their presence. For instance, the bar staff will need to ice the beverages and set up the bar, which takes time. The food servers, however, won't have anything to do early on; it's better to get them in 15 minutes before the guests are due to arrive and keep them on at the end for the clean-up.

Small and casual

For a more intimate party, and especially if you're organising the food yourself rather than getting a caterer, ask the hospitality staffing agency about the possibility of hiring a 'cook/serve'. This is a person who can do both tasks: they may be a waiter with a cheffing or food-preparation background or vice versa. You pay a little more for their expertise, but it saves you having to hire two staff, and frees you of both kitchen and serving duties.

If you're going to be away from the kitchen/serving area during the party, make sure you write a list of instructions for your staff. This should clearly set out presentation, cooking instructions and times, the order of events for the function, and when you'd like different items to be served. Also, clearly label the things the staff will be using and write down where they're located. Even if you're doing it all yourself, it still pays to write a list so that nothing gets forgotten.

If the bar will already be organised and the food trayed up, you may just want to get in a paid helper, someone hired to keep things in order and help with the dreaded clean-up. Here, there's usually little need for a full staff of professionals. You could try to get a student to help out or perhaps approach government employment agencies. Catering colleges are also great places to look, as students are always eager for experience.

Naturally, the cheapest staff of all are volunteers. But be a kind host. They'll want to enjoy the party too, so don't tie them up for the whole time. If you can muster the help of more than one friend, delegate specific tasks so that each person has only a brief helping-out stint.

Remember ... the golden rule when hiring staff is to make your basic requirements crystal clear. Then everyone concerned, guests included, will be happy.

Drinks

What to serve
You'll notice that each chapter in this book contains suggestions for serving drinks tailored to the occasion. These may be cocktails, punches or other drinks designed to enhance the atmosphere of your party. Served to each guest as they arrive, these drinks are great ice-breakers, if you'll pardon the pun. Not only do they give people something to chat about as they're introduced to each other, but they also set the tone of the party. For example, you could serve Moscow Mules (vodka, crushed ice, lime juice and ginger ale) for a winter gathering. You can of course serve them throughout, but most hosts will prefer to restrict them to the beginning and then serve more usual beverages.

In general, the most popular drinks at a party will be Champagne (or a good sparkling wine), white wine and beer (full strength and low alcohol). Red wine is more popular in the colder months. Always provide mineral water and orange juice for guests who do not want to drink alcohol.

How much to serve
There's nothing like good advice to smooth the ordering of drinks for a party. If a liquor store is taking care of your drinks service, ask them about quantities – they'll have the requisite knowledge to guide you towards what's good quality and good value.

Business is competitive nowadays, and most good liquor suppliers will offer a 'sale or return' facility. That is, you get a refund for unused stock, provided it's in the same condition as when you took delivery (that is, no scraped labels or damaged packaging). The merchant can then re-sell it. This is a fantastic service, particularly if you're not sure how much the crowd will consume. Even the weather can influence this, and I defy anyone to know that in advance!

A good supplier will deliver your beverages chilled and free of charge at the time you require. They should also have free tub and glass loan, although you'll have to pay for breakages and ice. Be sure to check whether glassware needs to be washed before it's returned or you may be charged extra.

Most people demand value for money, regardless of how big the budget is. When scouting for a liquor supplier, ring around to compare prices, discounts, deals and services. If a supplier falls short of your requirements – even one who's been recommended to you – it shouldn't be too difficult to find another that provides a full service. Unless you're in the business or are a keen observer of such matters, you probably won't know all the ins and outs of wine styles, vintages, quality and fair pricing. A reputable company should be able to guide you, and, if you throw parties often, try to develop an ongoing relationship with a supplier you trust.

You'll both benefit from each other's business.

Taking advantage of specials (discounted stock) is a great thing, but only if your guests will enjoy drinking it. A word to the wise: don't buy too cheap. The drinks you serve tend to set the mood for the party and will do little to complement the beautiful food you've made if they're second-rate. For some occasions it's appropriate to supply a really nice greeting drink and have guests bring other alcohol themselves, or to serve just a few basic tipples (wine, beer, soft drinks). Don't let a limited budget get in the way of a fun time!

Atmosphere

Food and drink are essential to a great party, but they're not the be-all and end-all. In fact, the atmosphere is what makes or breaks a party. What your guests consume are simply ingredients for it. So, while it's crucial to do the nibbles and drinks well, it pays to put a little thought into creating a sense of occasion. If you present your function, however small, as a total package, you'll reap the rewards.

Start by considering these basic points:
- The venue. What are its advantages and limitations? How can you decorate it to make the space convivial and reflect the theme of the party?
- Who are your guests? Obviously, the mood at a party thrown for close friends and family will be different from a gathering of business associates, for instance.
- Time of year. The seasons affect the way we feel. Do you need to tailor the occasion for steamy hot or freezing cold?
- Reason for the party. These are unlimited! Some affairs will have an overt sense of celebration (for example, a wedding or birthday), while other gatherings will be more low-key.

From there, work within your budget and make the effort to idealise your theme. A little styling can make all the difference to the success of your party. Put some thought into such things as the serving trays, lighting, dress code and music. You can even bump up the ambience by improving the smell of the room with scented candles and aromatherapy oil burners. Your vision for the occasion will be realised, giving you a sense of achievement and pride.

Choosing a menu

Type of food

I like to divide my menu into four main categories: meat, poultry, seafood and vegetarian. Provide equal quantities of each if possible.

Many people don't eat red meat or are vegetarians (and some of the latter, vegans, don't eat dairy products or eggs). If you feel you need to clarify this, say, if the party is small, you could always put a question on the invitation. When your guests reply, they will then let you know if they have any dietary constraints.

Variety stimulates the palate, so always create a good mix of textures. Mix crisp, baked foods with smooth, creamy fillings, and remember to create an interesting contrast of colours. I like to serve a variety of hot and cold nibbles, but of course that depends on the time of year. For instance, to create a warm and cosy feeling for a winter gathering, make the majority of the food hot. Conversely, summer is the perfect time to serve such treats as crisp, cool ices, chilled seafood and salad ingredients. Whatever the situation, the rule of thumb is to serve cold items first, as people are less likely to go back to cold morsels once they've eaten several hot ones.

Quantities

In my experience, hosts always have a tendency to over-cater. But with a little planning you can avoid having to eat party leftovers for days afterwards. Use the following as a guide:
- For a cocktail party, allow 8–12 canapés per head.

- For a function being held in place of lunch or dinner, allow 14–16 canapés per head.
- Assume that each guest will eat 1½–2 of each sort of canapé.
- A rule of thumb worth remembering is that the more guests in attendance, the less they will eat per head. This phenomenon may sound strange, but I have found it to be true. Conversely, the bigger the crowd, the more each guest tends to drink!

People will usually have had enough to eat after 2–2½ hours of food service. However, if you are having a party that will run late into the night, it's a good idea to serve a late-night snack, perhaps Singapore Barbecued Pork Noodle Boxes, leg ham rolls with mustard, or a cheese-and-fruit platter.

Ingredients

When you're planning your shopping list, always aim to achieve the best possible result with the least effort. For instance, if you need puff pastry but don't want to make it yourself, buy it from that terrific patisserie you know of. Sure, it may cost a little more and you may have to order it in advance, but the end result has an edge over frozen pastry from the supermarket. Likewise, buy the best olive oil and cheeses you can afford, and get premium-quality fresh pasta from a reputable maker.

There's no point skimping on quality when you're making party nibbles. Good ingredients make for intensity of flavour, texture and colour. Canapés are morsels, after all, so when guests choose one from the platter, you want them to experience a taste sensation. Don't forget, when you're putting on a party, you're on display, and people tend to remember a bad meal even more than they do a wonderful one.

party checklist

Use the following checklists in planning the big event. There's a lot to consider!

In the weeks and days leading up to the party.

One month before:
- Compile the guest list.
- Send the invitations, by post, fax, over the telephone or by e-mail.
- Organise the following: serving/cooking staff; someone to clean up; equipment hire; music; beverages (alcohol and soft drinks). Specify delivery times and ask for a letter of confirmation for what you have ordered.

Two weeks before:
- Plan the menu.
- Shop for the atmosphere you wish to create: for example, food trays, candles, flowers, table decorations – even a new outfit!
- Buy a disposable camera.

Three days before:
- Shop for food.
- Make the dishes that you are able to freeze, then pop them in the freezer.

On the day before the party:
- Make sure all the food preparation is done. The only cooking you should contemplate on the day is final assembly of components and putting things in the oven just before they're to be served.

On the day:
- Prepare an area for the return of dirty glasses.
- Arrange the flowers, candles, streamers or whatever you're decorating the room with.
- Prepare the bathroom.
- Rearrange/remove furniture to create more space.
- Warn the neighbours that you're having a party.
- Set up the bar. Remember to position it so that it won't cause bottlenecks in the room.
- Write instructions for staff.

Drinks equipment

Hire any equipment you don't have or if you don't wish to use your own.

- Glasses: Champagne flutes, highballs, wine glasses, cocktail/martini glasses, shot glasses
- Jugs for water and juice
- Drinks trays and cloths
- Table and tablecloth for the bar and/or buffet
- Bottle openers and corkscrews – at least three
- Paper cocktail serviettes
- Ice buckets and tongs
- Small chopping board and knife (for garnishes and so on)
- Appropriate garnishes and fruit for drinks, for example, lemons, limes, berries, mint leaves

party equipment

- Drinks accessories, if desired, such as swizzle sticks or other items suiting your theme
- Tubs for drinks and ice
- Something to protect the floor underneath the tubs
- Rubbish bags and bins
- Tea towels (kitchen towels) and wiping cloths
- Blender

Tea and coffee
- Teapots, if desired
- Kettle
- Coffee plungers
- Cups and saucers
- Teaspoons
- Sugar bowl
- Milk jug

House
- Serving trays
- Toilet paper
- Soap
- Air freshener

- Hand-towels in bathroom
- Candles and matches, birthday candles and sparklers if appropriate
- Dustpan and brush for breakages
- Ashtrays (you might want to consider allocating a smoking section, or politely request that guests smoke outside)

Kitchen equipment

Appliances:
- Food processor
- Blender
- Handheld electric mixer
- Electric spice grinder (an inexpensive coffee grinder will do)
- Pepper mill

Cutting and slicing tools:
- Good-quality stainless steel knives in various sizes
- Chinese cleaver for chopping
- Japanese steel cleaver for julienning and sashimi
- Chinese mandoline or small slicer
- Knife steel for sharpening
- Sturdy chopping boards (plastic and wood)
- Set of round pastry cutters
- Heart- and animal-shaped pastry cutters

Tins and baking items:
- Miniature muffin tins
- Miniature quiche tins
- Miniature terrine tins
- Tarlet tins (round- and flat-base)
- Small madeleine tray
- Flat metal baking trays
- Deep baking trays
- Blini pan
- Cooling rack
- Colanders
- Metal strainer
- Measuring spoons
- and cups
- Piping bags and nozzles
- Pastry brushes (large and small)
- Rubber spatula
- Metal spatula
- Rolling pin
- Wire whisks
- Tongs
- Tweezers (for removing fish bones)
- Grater
- Citrus zester
- 30 ml (1 fl oz) ladle
- Silicon paper

If travel broadens the mind, this is especially true for a chef. While a student, and subsequently a professional cook, I spent a considerable amount of time travelling the world, looking, tasting, discovering and learning. Today we have no qualms about taking the ingredients and techniques of other cultures and subtly using them for our own purposes: modern cuisine.

The beauty of canapés is that you can take a multitude of dishes from any cuisine you like and present them as a grand regional feast – in miniature. French, Italian and Asian cuisines are my definite favourites, and thus the ones I focus on here. But it's not just cultural differences that make the world so interesting, there's the passing of time to consider, too. That's why I've included sections called Contemporary and Retro.

In these, I've selected influences from my three main cuisines and adapted them to evoke the modern and the old-fashioned. For instance, in Contemporary there's a recipe that uses hash browns and avocado salsa (from the Americas) and another using salad ingredients with Japanese seaweed (the fusion of East and West). In Retro you'll find that vol au vents and fondues live on, as does rustic French country pâté.

Influences
Living, learning, adapting ...

French

The technical excellence of French cooking is second to none, and it's this level of skill and commitment that many professional chefs dream of achieving. In the following recipes I've sought to combine French regional flavours with Parisian panache. Serve them with a good French Champagne, rosé or Alsatian dry white.

Herb tuilles with brandade (left)
Brioche croûte with scallop mousse and Sauternes aspic (right front)

Makes 20

The tuilles

3 tbsp	plain (all-purpose) flour
3 tbsp	cornflour (cornstarch)
3 tbsp	butter
3	egg whites
¼	bunch chervil, coarsely chopped
10	chives, finely chopped
	spray oil

Preheat the oven to 180°C (350°F, gas mark 4).

Place the flour and cornflour in the bowl of a food processor, then add the butter and egg whites. Process for 30 seconds or until the mixture is well combined – it should resemble a fine, silky paste.

Add the chervil and chives. Whip for 10 seconds to incorporate the herbs, but no longer. It's good to retain some texture.

Spray a round-based 12 x 5 cm (2 in) mould tartlet tin with a liberal amount of olive oil.

Spoon a half-teaspoon of the herb mixture into each of the tartlet moulds. Using the back of a spoon, spread a thin layer of the mixture over the base and sides of the mould.

Place the tray in the oven and bake for 5 minutes or until the edges of the tuilles are golden brown.

The brandade

225 g	(7 oz) salt cod, soaked for 12 hours in several changes of water
⅓ cup	olive oil
⅓ cup	hot milk
	pinch of nutmeg and freshly ground white pepper
	juice of half a lemon

Place the cod in a saucepan of cold water and bring to the boil. Simmer for 10 minutes then drain the fish and set aside to cool. Remove the skin and bones, leaving just the flesh.

Flake the flesh with a fork and place in a medium-sized saucepan with one-quarter of the olive oil. Heat gently.

Mash the flesh into a purée while slowly adding the rest of the olive oil. Slowly add the hot milk, stirring until the mixture resembles mashed potatoes.

Season with the nutmeg, pepper and lemon juice to taste.

To serve, spoon a small amount of brandade into each tuille cup. Serve immediately, before the cases soften and collapse.

Herb tuilles with brandade

Makes 20

250 g (8 oz) sea scallops, cleaned, roe and
membranes removed
¼ cup Mayonnaise (see Master Recipe)
zest of half a lemon, finely grated
20 Brioche Croûtes (see Master Recipe)

Pan-fry the scallops for 30 seconds on each side, then set
aside to cool.
Combine the scallops, mayonnaise and lemon zest in the
bowl of a food processor.
Pulse-process the mix until the scallops form a paste with
the texture and appearance of fine breadcrumbs – well
combined but not too smooth.
Spoon a small amount of the seafood mixture onto each
croûte.
Top with a square of Sauternes aspic.

The Sauternes aspic
⅓ cup Sauternes or other late-harvest dessert wine
1 tbsp gelatine granules
1 tbsp cold water

Heat the wine to simmering in a small saucepan.
Mix the gelatine with the water and let stand for 30 seconds.
Remove the wine from heat and add the gelatine solution,
stirring until no granules remain.
Pour the jelly mixture into a small, flat-based container and
refrigerate until solid.
Turn the aspic jelly out of the mould and cut into squares.

Chef's Tip
The cooking time for scallops depends on their size. If
overdone they lose their succulence, so aim for a slightly
raw centre when you cook them.

Brioche croûte
with scallop
mousse and
Sauternes aspic

Makes 20

The bouillabaisse

1	eschalot (shallot or pickling onion), peeled and diced
1 tbsp	olive oil
4 cups	(1 L) Bouillon (see Master Recipe)
20	fresh surf clams, with shells
200 g	(6½ oz) good-quality miniature seafood mix containing mussels, prawns (shrimp), octopus, squid, scallops and clams, all evenly sized
1	egg (plum) tomato, finely diced
1	clove garlic, minced
¼ cup	mixed chopped dill and flat-leaf (Italian) parsley

Fry the eschalot in the oil until opaque. Set aside on absorbent paper.

Heat the bouillon in a large saucepan until simmering.

Add the clams and cook until the shells open.

Remove the clams from the liquid, allow to cool slightly, then snap each shell apart at the joint and remove the flesh. Return the bouillon to the heat.

Immerse the seafood mix in the bouillon and cook, stirring, until the pieces turn opaque, 30–60 seconds. Remove the seafood from the bouillon and set aside to cool.

Mix the seafood with the eschalot, tomato, clams, garlic and herbs.

The rouille

1	capsicum (pepper)
½ cup	Mayonnaise (see Master Recipe)
7	strands saffron

Preheat the oven to 220°C (425°F, gas mark 7).

Brush the capsicum with oil, then bake it in the oven, turning regularly until the skin blisters on all sides.

Transfer to a clean tea towel (kitchen towel) and rub gently to remove the skin. Cut open and remove the seeds.

Blend all ingredients in a food processor until smooth.

To serve, place spoonfuls of seafood in the half clam shells, then top with a small amount of rouille. Serve with small, disposable bamboo forks.

Chef's Tip

Freeze the cooking liquid for later use as a fish stock.

Miniature
bouillabaisse
shells with rouille

Makes 20

> 10 miniature pears
> 1 sheet ready-made puff pastry
> 60 g (2 oz) brie, chopped into small pieces

Preheat the oven to 200°C (400°F, gas mark 6).

Peel the miniature pears in downward strokes, starting at the tip and finishing at the base.

Cut the peeled pears lengthwise into halves or quarters, depending on the size of the pear – aim for bite-sized pieces.

Remove the seeds using a melon-baller.

Lay the pastry sheet on a lightly floured surface. Place the pear slices on the pastry and trace around each one with a knife, leaving a 3 mm (⅛ in) lip of pastry.

Place the individual pastries on a greased 23 cm (9 in) baking tray.

Bake for 15 minutes.

Remove from the oven and place a small segment of brie on each pastry.

Serve immediately; the brie will melt to form a glaze over the pear.

Chef's Tip

> If only standard-sized pears are available, cut these into quarters and shape them into miniature pears using a paring knife.
> Miniature pear pastries are quite versatile, and can be used as hors d'oeuvres, petits fours with coffee, or in place of dessert cheese and fruit.

Pear pastries glazed with brie

Italian

While the French have taught us the value of technical skill in the kitchen, the Italians have provided the gift of simple, satisfying food. More than any other culture, they have infiltrated our everyday eating habits, even if the fast-food version, the humble pizza, is a far cry from the original. What's their secret? It's all to do with a magical interaction of tradition and uncompromising insistence on quality, flavour and fresh ingredients.

Tuscany is a good starting point in planning an Italian party. For an alfresco soirée, decorate the table with grapes and vines. (For further inspiration, rent out Kenneth Branagh's film version of Shakespeare's 'Much Ado About Nothing', which is set in and around a Tuscan villa.) To accompany the food, go for a Chianti in a characteristic wicker-encased bottle, and serve the food on rustic terracotta platters. Or go all out, as I did recently, and create a lavish Venetian masked ball – an unforgettable experience. Here the ideal greeting drink is Peach Bellini, that classic Venetian cocktail invented at Harry's Bar in the 1950s and made with Champagne and fresh peach purée.

Crisp ravioli in basil aïoli

Baby stuffed mushrooms baked in vine leaves

Makes 20

For this recipe, visit a fresh pasta store and choose three different-coloured ravioli with tasty fillings. The examples used here are only a guide.

The ravioli

1¼ cups	vegetable oil, for frying
100 g	(3½ oz) saffron ravioli
100 g	(3½ oz) red capsicum (pepper) ravioli
100 g	(3½ oz) parsley ravioli

Heat the oil in a heavy saucepan or deep-fryer.
Deep-fry the ravioli, a few at a time, until they rise to the surface.
Drain on absorbent paper.
Serve immediately with the basil aïoli.

The basil aïoli

1 cup	basil leaves, tightly packed
1 tbsp	olive oil
½ cup	Mayonnaise (see Master Recipe)
3 drops	Tabasco sauce

Process the basil leaves in a food processor with the olive oil.
Pour in the mayonnaise and Tabasco and combine.

Chef's Tip

> Rather than coating the ravioli with sauce, serve the basil aïoli in a dipping bowl. I generally choose vegetarian fillings for the ravioli as it's a good way to give the vegetarians a bit of variety.

Crisp ravioli in
basil aïoli

Makes 20

1	eschalot (shallot or pickling onion), peeled and finely diced
1 tbsp	olive oil
⅓ cup	pine nuts, freshly dry-roasted
⅔ cup	goat's cheese ricotta (available from Continental food stores)
2 tbsp	grated good-quality Parmesan cheese (do not use pre-packaged grated cheese)
¼ cup	fresh oregano leaves, chopped
¼ cup	fresh flat-leaf (Italian) parsley leaves, chopped
20	medium-sized button mushrooms, stalks removed
20	medium-sized preserved vine leaves (available from Continental food stores)

Preheat oven to 220°C (425°F, gas mark 7).

Pan-fry the eschalot in the oil until opaque.

Mix the pine nuts, cheeses, eschalot and herbs in a small bowl.

Spoon about 1½ tablespoons of the mixture into the cavity of each mushroom.

Position each mushroom in the centre of a vine leaf.

Fold the edges of the vine leaf up around the sides of the mushroom to form a cup.

Repeat this procedure with the remaining mushrooms and vine leaves.

Place the parcels on a baking tray, making sure they are evenly spaced.

Bake in the oven for 15 minutes.

Serve hot.

Chef's Tip

The salt in the preserved vine leaves will turn crisp and white when cooked, giving an authentically rustic look.

Baby stuffed
mushrooms
baked in
vine leaves

Makes 20

2	cloves garlic, crushed
¼ cup	virgin olive oil, plus a little extra for basting
1 cup	breadcrumbs, preferably from a ciabatta loaf
6	ripe egg (plum) tomatoes
	Maldon (kosher) sea salt and freshly ground black pepper
4	bocconcini cheeses (small balls of fresh mozzarella)
½ cup	basil leaves, tightly packed
1	egg, lightly beaten
20	zucchini (courgette) flowers
1 tbsp	plain (all-purpose) flour
1 tbsp	grated Parmesan cheese (do not use pre-packaged grated cheese)

Preheat the oven to 220°C (425°F, gas mark 7).

Fry the garlic in the olive oil until a nutty brown colour.

Stir in the breadcrumbs until they are moistened in the oil.

Cut the tomatoes lengthwise into quarters, remove the seeds, then dice into ¼ cm (⅛ in) squares so that they will fit into the flowers. Season to taste with salt and pepper.

Dice the bocconcini into ½ cm (¼ in) squares.

Finely shred the basil.

Mix the breadcrumbs, tomato, bocconcini, basil and beaten egg together.

Place spoonfuls of the mixture in each flower, packing firmly, then close the petals around the opening.

Place on a lightly greased baking tray and repeat with the remaining flowers.

Brush the stuffed flowers with olive oil.

Combine the flour and the Parmesan, then dust the mix over each flower.

Bake in the oven for 10 minutes or until the stuffing firms and the tops are brown.

Serve warm, before the bocconcini become stringy.

Chef's Tip

These flowers are delicious as part of an antipasto platter.

Grilled zucchini flowers with bruschetta-style tomatoes and bocconcini

Potato, rosemary and virgin olive oil pizzas

Makes 20

6 chat (baby) potatoes, washed
1 sprig rosemary, needles only
virgin olive oil, for brushing
Maldon (kosher) sea salt and freshly ground pepper
20 squares Pizza Base (see Master Recipe)

Preheat the oven to 200°C (400°F, gas mark 6).
Slice the potatoes to transparent thickness using a Chinese mandoline slicer.
Chop the rosemary needles coarsely, then fold into the oil.
Brush the potato slices with the oil.
Arrange the pizza squares evenly on a lightly greased baking tray, then top each one with some of the potato.
Spoon a little more rosemary oil over the pizzas and sprinkle with sea salt and freshly ground black pepper.
Place in oven and bake for 15 minutes. The potato should be soft, with edges that are just turning brown.
Serve hot.

Chef's Tip

These little pizzas go down especially well in winter. I like to serve these with their fig, prosciutto and gorgonzola cousins, together, them in a chequerboard pattern on the platter.
Don't forget to use the guard on the mandoline slicer to avoid slicing your fingers.

Fig, prosciutto and gorgonzola pizzas

Makes 20

5 medium-sized ripe figs
60 g (2 oz) gorgonzola cheese, roughly chopped
10 slices prosciutto (parma ham)
20 squares Pizza Base (see Master Recipe)

Preheat the oven to 200°C (400°F, gas mark 6).
Cut the figs into quarters.
Insert a piece of gorgonzola into the centre of each fig segment.
Cut the prosciutto slices in half lengthwise, then securely wrap a strip around the cheese and fig.
Arrange the pizza squares on a lightly greased baking sheet, placing a prosciutto wrap on each square.
Bake in oven for 15 minutes.
Serve hot.

There are many different Asian cultures and even more variations in the ways their food is cooked. You can explore them all with the huge range of country-specific Asian cookbooks available, but what I've done for the following recipes is borrow a little from a few.

Asia has given us a mind-boggling diversity of flavours, textures and ingredients. It's taught us the best way to eat in a hot climate: about mixing sweet with sour (as in China); about the virtues of good, simple ingredients (Japan); and how to combine a range of fragrances and tastes (Thailand).

The vibrant appearance and intense flavours of the East are easy to utilise in a party. You could serve warmed sake in little Japanese ceramic cups for your greeting drink, then use glazed sushi platters and a variety of bamboo steamers for the food. Decorate the room with vivid red lanterns and inexpensive bamboo screens and you'll set an Eastern mood quickly and easily.

Asian

Wonton skins with Thai duck curry sauce

Sashimi tuna and daikon radish wrapped in crispy soba noodles

Makes 20

The duck curry sauce

1 x 500 g (1 lb)	duck, roasted
½ cup	thick coconut milk
1½ tbsp	Thai red curry paste
½ cup	thin coconut milk
2	small kaffir lime leaves
½ tbsp	palm sugar (available from Asian food stores)
2	cardamom pods, bruised
½	eggplant (aubergine) cut into 1/4 cm (1/8 in) dice
10 tbsp	ground, roasted peanuts or crunchy peanut butter
1 tbsp	fish sauce
1 tbsp	tamarind liquid
½ tbsp	lime juice

Shred the duck into bite-sized pieces.

Heat half of the thick coconut milk, stir in the curry paste and cook for 10 minutes until fragrant, stirring constantly.

Add the duck pieces, the thin coconut milk, kaffir lime leaves, palm sugar and cardamom pods. Simmer for 30 minutes.

Stir in the eggplant, peanuts/peanut butter and the remaining thick coconut milk. Cook for a further 10 minutes.

Add the fish sauce, tamarind liquid and lime juice to the curry sauce, and simmer until reduced by one-quarter.

The wonton cups

20	wonton wrappers
1 cup	canola or other vegetable oil
30 ml (1 fl oz)	ladle

Trim the stack of wonton wrappers to make 4 cm x 4 cm (1½ in x 1½ in) squares, then separate into individual sheets.

Heat the oil and press a wonton wrapper onto the outside of a 30 ml (1 fl oz) ladle.

Immerse the ladle in the hot oil until the wonton wrapper is lightly browned and crisp. The wrapper will now be a bowl shape. Drain on absorbent paper.

Repeat this procedure until all the wonton wrappers have been deep-fried.

To serve, place the duck mixture in the wonton cups and serve immediately.

Chef's Tip

You can easily make this a vegetarian dish by replacing the duck with vegetables such as pumpkin and cauliflower.

Wonton skins with Thai duck curry sauce

Makes 20

300 g (9½ oz) sashimi-quality tuna
2 tsp wasabi powder
5 cm (2 in) length of daikon radish (a white radish, available from Asian food stores)
60 g (2 oz) pickled ginger
2 sheets nori (Japanese seaweed)
100 g (3½ oz) soba noodles, cooked al dente
1 cup canola or other vegetable oil, for deep-frying

Cut the tuna into 2 cm (¾ in) squares.
Dust lightly with the wasabi powder.
Peel the daikon radish, then shred finely using a Chinese mandoline slicer.
Julienne the ginger very finely, again with the mandoline.
Roll up the nori sheets and julienne them just as finely as the ginger – you will need a very sharp knife for this, or use a Chinese cleaver.
Combine the daikon with the ginger and nori.
Using the palm of your hand, fashion 2 tablespoons of this mixture into a round patty.
Place a piece of the tuna in the centre, then enclose it in the daikon mixture to make a ball.
Take a few strands of soba noodles and wind them around the ball of tuna, much as you would string. Don't completely cover the ball – just enough to secure the daikon does the trick.
Heat the canola oil in a saucepan. When it reaches boiling point, turn the heat down by half.
Immerse the tuna balls in the oil for 10 seconds or until the noodles turn crispy.
Serve hot.

Chef's Tip

These morsels can be prepared up to one day in advance. Keep them in an airtight container lined with cling film and cook just before serving.

Sashimi tuna and daikon radish wrapped in crispy soba noodles

Makes 20

1	iceberg lettuce, washed
100 g	(3½ oz) minced (ground) chicken
100 g	(3½ oz) minced (ground) lean pork
1	egg yolk
1 tbsp	rice flour
2 tbsp	rice wine
	Maldon (kosher) sea salt and freshly ground black pepper
⅓ cup	water chestnuts
¼ cup	shiitake mushrooms
1 cup	canola or other vegetable oil, for frying
½ cup	chicken stock
1 tbsp	dark soy sauce
1 tsp	sesame oil
60 g	(2 oz) cellophane noodles

Baby sang choy bao with pork and water chestnuts

Cut circles 6 cm (2½ in) in diameter from the iceberg lettuce leaves.

Thoroughly mix the pork and chicken minces with the egg yolk, rice flour and rice wine, and season with salt and pepper.

Coarsely chop the water chestnuts and mushrooms, then stir through the mince mixture.

Heat a small amount of the canola oil in a frying pan and sauté the mixture for 5 minutes.

Pour in the stock, soy and sesame oil and simmer for a further 5 minutes or until the mixture absorbs the liquid.

Heat the remaining canola oil in a clean frying pan and deep-fry the cellophane noodles for 30 seconds or until white and crisp. Drain on paper towels.

Mix the noodles into the mince mixture.

To serve, place a little pile of mince mixture at the centre of each lettuce round.

Chef's Tip

Store the lettuce cups in cold water to keep them crisp until required.

To make these ahead of time, keep the lettuce, mince and noodles separate, and assemble just before serving.

Makes 20

20 Tempura Coconut Fritters
500 g (1 lb) beef fillet, whole
1 tsp chopped garlic
6 coriander (cilantro) roots
½ tsp green peppercorns
1 tbsp palm sugar (available from Asian food stores)
1 tbsp kecap manis (Indonesian sweet soy sauce)
1 tbsp lime juice
1 tbsp Thai fish sauce
2 eschalots (shallots or pickling onions)
1 red chilli, deseeded and julienned
1 stalk lemongrass
Green Mango Salsa (see Master Recipe)

Thai beef salad on tempura coconut fritters with green mango salsa

The tempura coconut fritters
⅓ cup tempura flour
¼ cup dry-roasted coconut flakes
⅔ cup coconut milk

Mix the tempura flour with the coconut flakes. Stir in the coconut milk and combine.

Drop tablespoonfuls of the batter onto a hot grill and brown on both sides.

Remove from the grill and keep warm.

Char-grill the beef fillet on a hotplate until cooked rare, about 10 minutes on each side. Rest the meat for 10 minutes.

Carve the fillet into wafer-thin slices.

Combine the garlic, coriander roots, green peppercorns and palm sugar in a food processor for about 1 minute.

Add the kecap manis, lime juice and fish sauce and combine until smooth.

Slice the eschalots, chilli and the lemongrass stalks wafer thin, then toss through the beef.

Pour the palm-sugar mixture over the beef and marinate for 30 minutes.

Lightly fold together the beef salad and the green mango salsa.

To serve, spoon the beef and mango mix onto the fritters.

Chef's Tip

These will stand for an hour before service. You can also prepare each component the day before and assemble just before serving.

Pre-cut cucumber cups can be substituted for the tempura coconut fritters. Store them in chilled water.

If there's one word that perfectly characterises the development of contemporary dining, it's 'fusion'. First to emerge from France in the 1970s was nouvelle cuisine, with its echoes of Japan and China, tiny, refined portions and obsession with presentation. And over the past few decades there's been a redefining of other traditional European national cuisines to accommodate ingredients and techniques from other parts of the globe. It's a sort of alchemy. This coming together of cuisines has certainly been popular (witness the extensive usage of the words 'modern' and 'new' in the vocabulary of contemporary cooking). While the originals will hopefully never disappear, it's exciting to witness the

Contemporary

evolution of age-old culinary standbys.

But what of the poor old canapé? While all this change was going on, it almost languished into obscurity. But hors d'oeuvres are perfectly adaptable to this 'new', 'modern' sensibility. Here I have used some newly in-vogue ingredients, as well as a few old ones, twisting them into witty, bite-sized versions of the contemporary ethos. Remember, minimalism is the key for a party with a contemporary theme. Pare down the decorations to the essentials, using simple, strong lines and bright, shiny colours. You could also think about stipulating stylish simplicity for the dress code.

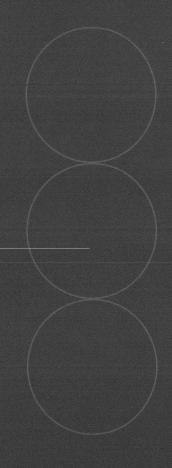

Crab with baby corn salsa in husk boats

Thai chicken and lime salad in noodle tarts with chilli jam

	juice of 1 lime
1 tbsp	sweet chilli sauce
½ cup	cooked crab meat
1	ear of corn, husks carefully removed and set aside
1 tbsp	corn oil
½ cup	purple basil, finely shredded
4 green	onions (spring onions or scallions), finely sliced
½ cup	coriander (cilantro) leaves, finely shredded

Pour the lime juice and sweet chilli sauce over the crab.
Fold together lightly without breaking up the crab too much.
Slice the corn kernels off the cob and sauté in the corn oil until browned.
Fold the corn and herbs together, then add to the crab. Again, be careful not to break up the crab too much.
To make the boats, cut the corn husks into 20 strips, 2 cm (¾ in) wide, plus 20 thin strips to use as ties. Some husks closer to the cob won't need cutting at all.
Create a boat shape from the corn husks by looping and tying a strip of husk 5 cm (2 in) up from the base of each.
Fill the cavity with the crab mixture and serve.

Chef's Tip

If preparing this recipe in advance, cover the husk boats with a damp tea towel (kitchen towel) to stop them drying out.

Use only the freshest corn for this recipe.

Crab with baby corn salsa in husk boats

Makes 20

100 g (3½ oz) kataifi (kadaif) pastry or finely shredded
filo (phyllo) pastry
olive oil cooking spray
Lime Leaf Chicken (see Master Recipe)
Chilli Jam (see Master Recipe)

Preheat the oven to 180°C (350°F, gas mark 4).
Pull apart the pastry and roll into 20 balls.
Coat miniature non-stick muffin-tin moulds with the olive oil cooking spray.
Press the pastry balls into the tins to form a tartlet shape. Make sure there is a cavity in the centre but that the base is covered.
Spray the pastry lightly with more oil.
Bake in the oven for 5 minutes. The tartlets should be golden and the pastry threads holding together.
Fill with Lime Leaf Chicken.
Top with Chilli Jam.

Chef's Tip

These little tarts are so easy! And because they look delicate and fiddly, they're just the thing to impress at parties. Don't fill the tart cases with wet filling more than 15 minutes before serving or the pastry threads will turn soggy.

Thai chicken
and lime salad in
noodle tarts with
chilli jam

Makes 20

The hash browns

1	small onion, chopped
1 tbsp	oil, for frying
1 kg	(2 lb) sweet potato, boiled in the skin until soft
¼ cup	potato flour (available from health-food stores)
3	eggs
1 cup	flat-leaf (Italian) parsley, leaves coarsely chopped

Preheat the oven to 220°C (425°C, gas mark 7).

Fry the onion in the oil until opaque. Remove from the pan and drain on absorbent paper.

Remove the skin from the sweet potato and discard. Combine the sweet potato flesh with the onion, flour, eggs and parsley.

Press heaped teaspoons of the potato mixture into miniature non-stick muffin-tin moulds. Ensure there is a generous well in the centre of each hash brown to accommodate the filling.

Bake for 15–20 minutes or until the mixture has slightly browned and comes away easily from the sides of the tin.

The beef chilli

½	small onion, finely diced
1 tbsp	canola or other vegetable oil, for frying
⅛ tsp	chilli powder
¼ tsp	each of ground cumin and ground coriander
250 g	very lean minced (ground) beef
⅓ cup	paprika relish
1 tbsp	olive oil, for browning
	salt and freshly ground black pepper

Sauté the onion in the canola oil until opaque. Add the spices to the onion and stir over high heat for 30 seconds.

Brown the mince in the same pan as the onion and spices until it separates easily, without lumps.

Add the paprika relish and simmer for a further 20 minutes.

Season with salt and pepper to taste.

The avocado salsa

	juice of 1 lime
1	egg (plum) tomato, finely diced
1	firm, ripe avocado, seed removed, flesh finely diced
1	cup chopped fresh coriander (cilantro) leaves

Pour the lime juice over the tomato and avocado. Add the coriander and toss lightly to combine.

To assemble, place a heaped teaspoon of beef chilli on each hash brown and top with ½ teaspoon salsa.

Sweet-potato hash browns with beef chilli and avocado salsa

Makes 20

5	sheets nori (Japanese seaweed)
¼ cup	baby rocket (arugula) leaves
¼ cup	enokitake (enoki) mushrooms
20	ears baby corn
1	serve Marinated Vegetables (see Master Recipe)
1	serve Peanut Paste (see Master Recipe)
20	ears baby corn
1 tbsp	mirin (sweet Japanese rice vinegar)
1 tbsp	dark soy sauce
1 tsp	sesame oil
½ tsp	wasabi powder

Nori salad rolls with marinated vegetables and peanut paste

Cut the nori in half lengthwise and lay 5 half-sheets on the bench, well spaced apart.

Arrange the rocket on the nori sheets with leaves protruding from each side.

Place the enokitake mushrooms on top of the rocket, with the mushroom caps protruding from each side.

Arrange the baby corn in the same fashion.

Top with the Marinated Vegetables and Peanut Paste.

Mix together the mirin, soy, sesame oil and wasabi powder. Brush the remaining nori sheets with this mixture and lay them brushed-side down over the top of each filled sheet.

Press down on the nori sheets and roll them up away from you, keeping each turn very tight until complete.

Cut through the middle of each roll, then stand each half on its flat end to get the effect of little flower pots.

Chef's Tip

To make these from scratch can take a little work but if you prepare the master recipes ahead of time it only takes minutes.

Prepare the rolls 30 minutes before needed.

If a roll breaks, wrap another half-sheet of nori around it.

Retro

As the song goes, 'everything old is new again'. It's no surprise, then, that mothers everywhere are continually asked for their party recipes by children leaving home. In fact, we have our mothers to thank for the practice of serving nibbles at drinks parties in the first place. Probably, though, most of these women would be amused to know that, in passing down their wisdom, 'old-fashioned' cooking is being kept alive under a new banner: Retro.

I don't think a lot of people realise that, in the context of canapés and hors d'oeuvres, what we call 'retro' is actually what's remained fashionable ever since the advent of the 'cocktail era' in the 1950s and 1960s. But it's my belief that, in the kitchen at least, individuality is paramount, so don't be afraid to take flight when you're catering for a party.

With these recipes I've sought to take the kitsch out of some old favourites, to make them appeal to people of any age. The perfect party drink is a classic martini made from best-quality gin or vodka, and shaken or stirred as you like. A retro party is also a great opportunity to dress up, both the room and the bodies in it. They say fashion goes in 20-year cycles, and at the moment quite a few clothing labels are producing items that you'd swear were designed decades ago. Otherwise, check out the thrift stores, where you can also usually find suitable, inexpensive serving trays, punch bowls and ornaments for decorating. A room full of pant-suits, halter-neck frocks, frilly Tom Jones shirts, plastic fruit and wood-grain trimming can really take you back!

Coarse pâté with country-style hollandaise on brioche croûtes (left)
Baby vol au vents with chicken and crispy leek (right)

Makes 20

The vol au vents

3   sheets ready-made puff pastry, dividing paper removed and pastry sheets placed one on top of the other
1   egg yolk

Preheat the oven to 200°C (400°F, gas mark 6).
Cut the pastry into 3 cm (1¼ in) squares and place on a greased tray.
Brush the surface evenly with a thin film of the egg yolk.
With the tip of a small knife, cut an inner square ½ cm (¼ in) from the edge. Cut only halfway through the pastry, and do not remove at this stage.
Bake for 15 minutes or until well risen and golden.
When cool, cut carefully around the inner square and ease out the pastry.
Scrape away any uncooked pastry from the centre so there is plenty of room for the filling.

The chicken mixture

½   medium-sized leek, white section only, finely diced
1 tbsp   oil
1 cup   dry white wine
200 g   (6½ oz) uncooked chicken breast, finely diced
2 cups   pouring (single) cream
¼ cup   tarragon leaves
salt and freshly ground black pepper
½ tbsp   potato flour (available from health-food stores)
2 tbsp   cold water
200 g   (6½ oz) uncooked chicken breast, finely diced
Crispy Leek (see Master Recipes)

Preheat the oven to 180°C (350°F, gas mark 4).
Fry the leek in oil until slightly opaque and soft but not brown.
Pour in the wine and simmer for 5 minutes or until the liquid has reduced by one-third.
Add the cream and tarragon, and again reduce by simmering for 5 minutes or until slightly syrupy. Season to taste.
Whisk the potato flour with the water, then add to the mixture.
Remove from the heat, then add the chicken.
Fill the vol au vents with the mixture and bake in the oven until the chicken is completely cooked, about 10 minutes.
Serve topped with the crispy leek.

Baby vol au vents with chicken and crispy leek

Makes 20

The pâté

1	eschalot (shallot or pickling onion), finely chopped
1	clove of garlic, crushed
2 tbsp	butter
250 g	(8 oz) duck livers, fat and membranes removed
2 tbsp	butter, softened
2 tbsp	brandy
1	sprig lemon thyme, leaves only
	salt and freshly ground black pepper.
½	serve Hollandaise Sauce (see Master Recipe)
20	Brioche Croûtes (see Master Recipe)
	extra lemon thyme leaves, for garnish

Cook the eschalot and garlic in the butter until opaque.

Remove from the pan and set aside.

Add the livers to the pan and brown on each side, leaving the centres pink.

Combine the onion mixture and the livers in a food processor and process for 30 seconds, gradually adding the lemon thyme leaves, softened butter and brandy.

Season to taste.

Process until combined well.

Transfer to a container and refrigerate.

To serve, spoon 1 teaspoon of the pâté onto each croûte.

Using the back of a spoon, make an indentation in the top of the pâté.

Whisk 3 tablespoons of pâté into the hollandaise sauce.

Spoon this mixture into the indentations in the pâté.

Garnish with 2–3 leaves of lemon thyme.

Coarse pâté with country-style hollandaise on brioche croûtes

Chef's Tip

The pâté will keep for up to a week in the refrigerator topped with clarified butter.

Don't put the pâté on the croûtes until just before serving or they will soften.

Makes 20

The cocktail sauce

1 cup	Mayonnaise (see Master Recipe)
	juice of 1 lemon
3 tbsp	good-quality Tomato Sauce (see Master Recipe)
¼ tsp	chilli powder
1	clove garlic, crushed
3 tbsp	horseradish relish
1 tbsp	brandy

Stir the mayonnaise and lemon juice together.
Whisk in the tomato sauce and chilli powder, then the remaining ingredients.

The prawns

500 g	(1 lb) uncooked small prawns (shrimp), peeled and deveined
4 cups	(1 L) Bouillon (see Master Recipe)
20	heart leaves of butter (butterhead) lettuce (about 3 lettuces)

Cook the prawns according to the Bouillon master recipe.
Cool the prawns and coat lightly with the cocktail sauce.
Carefully spoon the prawns into the lettuce cups.

Prawn cocktails in lettuce cups

Chef's Tip

Choose lettuces with tight centres as you only use the very small inside leaves.
To serve, use a martini glass for a full retro look.
Serve with wooden forks if the prawns are very small.

Makes 20

The fondue

    1 cup dry white wine
1 clove garlic, crushed
  1 tbsp potato flour (available from health-food stores)
  2 tbsp cold water
    1 cup grated gruyère cheese (do not use pre-packaged grated cheese)
    1 cup grated cheddar cheese (do not use pre-packaged grated cheese)

Heat the wine and garlic in a thick-bottomed saucepan until almost boiling.
Whisk the potato flour with the water, add to the saucepan and turn the heat to low. Stir continuously for 2 minutes or until the wine mixture becomes syrupy.
Remove from the heat and gradually add the cheeses, whisking constantly until smooth.
Serve immediately, keeping the fondue warm over a low burner.

Chef's Tip

    Use a good-quality dry white wine such as a riesling, as it carries the flavour.
    Add the cheese slowly to prevent it from curdling.

The prosciutto and cornichons

  20 bamboo sticks or fondue forks
  10 thin slices of prosciutto (parma ham), sliced in half lengthwise
  40 cornichons (baby gherkins, available from Continental food stores)

Thread a slice of prosciutto onto each bamboo skewer or fondue stick.
Add one cornichon, then a fold of prosciutto, another cornichon, then a final fold of prosciutto.
Arrange around the fondue burner and serve.

Chef's Tip

    Be careful not to overheat the fondue, as the cheese will become stringy.
    Borrow your mother's fondue set. And don't double dip!

Hot cheese fondue with prosciutto and cornichons

In the not-so-distant past there were no such things as supermarkets or Internet home-delivery services. Believe it or not, people would go to the market.

With a bag on one arm and a pointing finger on the other, you'd have a good look around, searching for the best fresh ingredients. Instead of demanding constant, year-round availability of produce, customers would choose the best of the moment, something freshly harvested, in the prime of seasonality and most likely organically grown.

The ancient institution that is the market is also a boon for modern cooks. People are greedy for interesting flavours, and places such as growers' markets are great

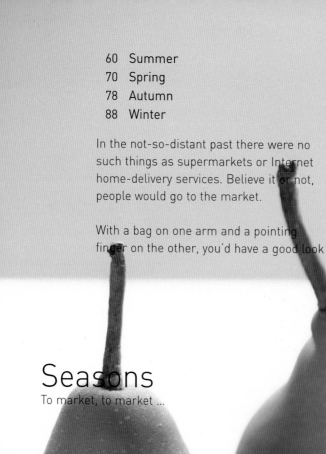

Seasons
To market, to market ...

places to obtain them. Here you can actively seek out old favourites as well as new varieties of fruit and vegetables. Produce from other cultures, now grown on home turf, can be sampled. People can delight in ingredients produced without chemicals, and not be too bothered by a perfectly natural blemish on a piece of fruit. If you live in or are visiting the country, don't forget to take advantage of 'gate sales', where fresh produce is sold directly. Just keep your eyes on the look-out for the homemade signs as you drive along. Best of all, whether market or farm outlet, you can usually talk about what's on offer with the person who's actually grown it. You don't get that in a shopping mall.

Whether it's Summer, Spring, Autumn or Winter, the recipes in this section are a celebration of the seasons. They're evidence of the passing of the year. What's good this month may be gone the next!

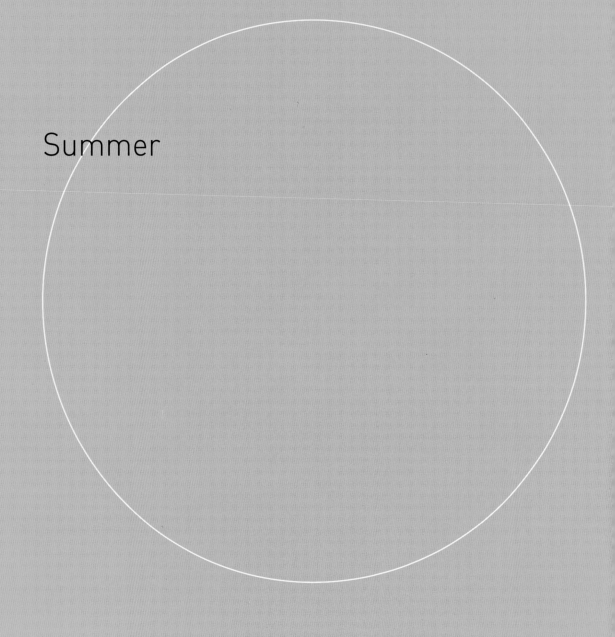

'Outside!' It's one catchcry of summer, quickly followed by 'Party!'. If you find yourself by the water for an occasion, then lucky you, but a park, balcony or the garden are terrific party locations, too. The following recipes were created for the barbecue, that icon of summer, but a little Korean hibachi grill will still do the trick.

Even if the summers where you live aren't really so hot, it still pays to create a summery setting. Encourage a holiday feel by using bright sarongs as tablecloths and cheap, contemporary bamboo platters to serve. Line them with lots of oiled banana leaves and you'll have everyone thinking they're on Gilligan's Island. Tropical

Summer

arrangements or even a mass of bright red chillies look stunning as table decorations.

Be sure to take advantage of the gorgeous berries available in summer. For instance, make a punch with sparkling white wine, sparkling burgundy and cranberry juice to taste, float some raspberries, strawberries and fresh mint on top, and ladle it into a big glass jug. Pretty to look at, this is also light and delicious and the perfect tipple for a radiant summer.

Sesame-crusted scallops

Gazpacho aspic with mustard ice cream

Makes 20

20	large sea scallops in the shell
¼ cup	coriander seeds
¼ cup	cumin seeds
⅔ cup	sesame seeds
¼ cup	uncooked hazelnuts
½ tbsp	Maldon (kosher) sea salt
½ tbsp	freshly ground black pepper
	butter, for barbecuing

Sesame-crusted scallops

Remove the scallops from their shells and cut off the white sinew. Rinse the scallops under running water and dry with absorbent paper. Set aside.

For the coating, dry-roast the coriander and cumin seeds in a small saucepan, then coarsely grind.

Dry-roast the sesame seeds until lightly browned, then coarsely grind.

Dry-roast the hazelnuts until the skin blisters. Enclose in a clean tea towel (kitchen towel) and rub roughly to remove the skin. Grind the hazelnuts to coarse crumbs.

Combine the ground ingredients in a bowl.

Roll each scallop thoroughly in the mixture until completely covered, then place each scallop back into a half shell.

Place a small dab of butter in each shell.

Barbecue the scallops in their shells for 30 seconds on each side, turning them in their shells.

Chef's Tip

Use large sea scallops as the coating will overpower the subtle flavour of smaller scallops.

Scallops should be quite firm to the touch They're best if they haven't been soaked in water and ice to plump them up.

Makes 20

½ onion, finely chopped
1 clove garlic, finely chopped
½ small chilli, seeded and chopped
1 tbsp olive oil
salt and freshly ground black pepper
1 tbsp sugar
2 cups tomato juice
3 tbsp paprika relish (available from Continental food stores) or roasted capsicum (pepper)
3 tbsp gelatine powder
2 tbsp cold water
½ tbsp tarragon, finely chopped
½ tbsp chives, finely chopped
½ tbsp flat-leaf (Italian) parsley, finely chopped
1 tbsp tarragon vinegar
½ small cucumber, finely grated
20 x 3 cm (1¼ in) square Brioche Croûtes (see Master Recipe)
Mustard Ice Cream (see Master Recipe)

Gazpacho aspic with mustard ice cream

Fry the onion, garlic and chilli in the olive oil until soft.
Add the tomato juice and season with salt, pepper and sugar.
Reduce by simmering for 10 minutes.
Puree the onion and tomato juice mixture in a blender, adding the paprika relish or capsicum.
Soak the gelatine in the water in a 15 cm (6 in) container for 30 seconds and dissolve it in the microwave for 1 minute on High (it will rise to about 4 times its volume).
Add the hot gelatine to the puree with the blender running.
Allow to cool for 10 minutes.
Transfer the mixture to a bowl, then add the herbs, vinegar and cucumber.
Pour into a shallow baking tray and refrigerate until set.
Cut the firm gazpacho aspic evenly into 2 cm (¾ in) cubes.
Place each cube on a croûte of about the same size.
Use a melon-baller to scoop a small well in the centre of the aspic.
Fill the well with mustard ice cream and serve immediately, before the ice cream melts.

The chermoula

3	cloves garlic
½ cup	mint leaves, coarsely chopped
1 cup	flat-leaf (Italian) parsley leaves, coarsely chopped
1 cup	coriander (cilantro) leaves and roots, coarsely chopped
2	green onions (spring onions or scallions)
1	fresh, small red chilli
	zest of 1 preserved lemon
½ cup	extra virgin olive oil
½ tsp	ground paprika
½ tsp	ground cumin
½ tsp	ground coriander
	salt and freshly ground black pepper

Combine the garlic, mint, parsley, coriander, shallots, chilli, lemon zest and half the oil in a food processor for 1 minute.
Add the spices and the remaining oil.
Season to taste.

Prawns in chermoula

Chef's Tip

When making sauces from leaf herbs, make sure that the blade of your food processor is sharp. If it isn't, you'll bruise and discolour the herbs.

The prawns

20	uncooked large prawns (shrimp), peeled and deveined, tails left on

Coat the prawns in the chermoula 30 minutes before required and cook for 1 minute each side on the barbecue.

Makes 20

With thanks to Paul Del Grande for help devising this recipe

> 20 toothpicks
> 20 river oysters or Sydney rock oysters
> ⅓ cup dark soy sauce
>   wasabi paste, to taste
> 2 tbsp pickled ginger, finely julienned
>   Crispy Leek (see Master Recipe)

Place a toothpick into the muscle (the tip end) of each oyster.
Mix the soy and wasabi paste together thoroughly. Serving lumps of wasabi won't make you any friends!
Drizzle 1 teaspoon of the mixture over each oyster.
Serve topped with pickled ginger and crispy leek.

Chef's Tip

For this particular recipe it is important to use small, intensely flavoured river-cultivated oysters, rather than ocean varieties.
You'll be amazed at the non-oyster eaters who'll be tempted by this recipe. The soy and wasabi combination works with raw fish, too, but use good soy.

Oysters

Spring

Most of us are glad to say goodbye to winter for another year, so a springtime party always goes down well. Even if there's no actual occasion to celebrate, the departure of grey skies, the onset of longer days and the donning of lighter clothing are excuse enough for a get-together.

And it's a great time for other reasons, too. The new season's fruit and vegetables are delicious, perfect for making into something good for your guests. Everything seems to sparkle in the sunlight, so take advantage of the new spring flowering bulbs when decorating your party. Bursting with colour, they brighten up the house and make a vibrant display when teamed with new green leaves and the blossoms of other plants.

For spring, go for brightly coloured drinks, perhaps blood-orange juice with vodka, Harvey Wallbangers, even mint julep. Serve your food on boldly coloured platters for maximum effect, ban the wearing of black at the gathering, and smell the fresh spring air.

Vitello tonnato (left)
Lamb souvlaki (right)

Makes 20

100 g	(3½ oz) lamb backstrap or loin roll
2	cloves garlic, crushed
	juice of 1 lemon
1 tbsp	olive oil
20	baby rocket (arugula) leaves
20	square Pizza Bases (see Master Recipe)
1	serve Tzatziki (see Master Recipe)
2	radishes, sliced to transparent thickness on a Chinese mandoline slicer

Lamb souvlaki

Remove the sinew from the lamb backstrap, being careful not to take off too much of the meat.

Marinate in the garlic, lemon juice and olive oil for 30 minutes.

Char-grill the lamb to medium pinkness on the barbecue, about 5 minutes on each side.

Remove from the grill and leave to rest for 15 minutes to seal in the juices.

Slice the lamb into thin slices across the grain.

Place 1 rocket leaf on each pizza base.

Top with a slice of lamb.

Spoon ¼ teaspoon of tzatziki onto the lamb and garnish with two slices of radish.

Chef's Tip

If you want to make the pizza base a day ahead, prepare the master recipe to pre-baking stage on trays, cover with cling wrap and place in the refrigerator. The chilling prevents the yeast from rising further. Bring to room temperature before cooking.

The tonnato sauce

	juice of ½ lemon
100 g	(3½ oz) tinned tuna, in oil
⅓ cup	Mayonnaise (see Master Recipe)
2 tbsp	baby capers

Blend the lemon juice and tuna in a food processor, then add the mayonnaise and 1 tablespoon of the capers until fully combined.

The veal

	(3½ oz) veal fillet
100 g	(3½ oz) veal fillet
20	Potato Galettes (see Master Recipe)

Preheat the oven to 220°C (425°F, gas mark 7).
Bake the veal to medium-rare in the oven for 10 minutes.
Allow to rest for 10 minutes before carving.
Slice the cooled veal thinly.
Place 1 piece of veal on each potato galette.
Drizzle the tonnato sauce over so you can still see the rare veal at the edges.
Garnish with the remaining baby capers.

Chef's Tip

This recipe is an adaptation of the classic Italian dish. The baby capers are a delicacy in themselves and provide less of a salt-hit than larger capers.

Vitello tonnato

Makes about 20

1	large leek, cut into 1 cm (⅓ in) rounds
2 tbsp	olive oil
6	large, ripe egg (plum) tomatoes, both ends discarded, cut into 1 cm (⅓ in) rounds
¼ cup	butter
1	serve Lemon Pistou (see Master Recipe)
2	sheets ready-made puff pastry

Preheat the oven to 220°C (425°F, gas mark 7).

Sauté the leek rounds in half the oil until lightly coloured on both sides but still holding their shape.

Repeat the same process with the tomatoes.

Butter a tray of medium-sized tartlet tins.

Place 1 round of leek and then 1 of tomato, alternating with 1 round of tomato and 1 of leek, in the moulds.

Spoon a teaspoon of lemon pistou over the vegetables.

Cut 5 cm (2 in) circles of puff pastry to use as lids and place on top.

Grease the underneath of another baking tray.

Place the second baking tray on top of the tartlets to hold the puff pastry down.

Bake in the oven for 15 minutes.

Allow to cool slightly, then invert the trays and remove the tartlet tin.

Serve vegetable side up.

Chef's Tip

On the serving tray, alternate the colours of the pale green leek and the tomatoes to create a chequerboard effect.

Leek and tomato tatins with lemon pistou

Makes 24

4   sheets nori (Japanese seaweed), cut in half lengthwise then into three crosswise

24   mizuna leaves or if unavailable, use young rocket (arugula) leaves

2 tbsp   wasabi mayonnaise (mix ¼ tsp wasabi paste and a few drops of lemon juice into 2 tbsp Mayonnaise – see Master Recipe)

1   serve Sugar-cured Trout (see Master Recipe)

2 tbsp   orange flying-fish roe (available from Japanese food stores)

20   garlic chives with flowers

soy sauce, for sealing

Sugar-cured trout in nori cones

Take one piece of the cut nori and lay it flat in front of you, horizontally.

Place 1 mizuna leaf diagonally across the nori from the centre out to top right.

Drizzle a small amount of mayonnaise over the mizuna leaf and top with cured-trout slices and flying-fish roe.

Add a chive with the flower protruding over the top edge of the nori.

Wet the edge of the nori with a small amount of soy.

Fold the right near corner of the nori over the filling, using your finger to roll it into a cone shape and seal tightly.

Chef's Tip

Prepare all the ingredients in advance but only assemble the cones 30 minutes before serving or the nori will become soft and discoloured.

Autumn

The golden afternoons of autumn are just right for alfresco parties. The sun has a certain warmth, but it's not the burning heat of summer or the uncanny brightness of spring. In short, it's just right, and you'll be glad to be out in it, given that winter's just around the corner.

Produce harvested in the autumn is at its ripest, sun-kissed best. It screams to be eaten, cooked or raw, and provides one last opportunity for warmer-weather fare before the cold really sets in. Autumn is a relaxing time, perfect for getting together with friends and family.

Forest mushroom and marscapone tarts

One of my autumn favourites is to mount a 'first crush' party. This celebrates the pressing of the year's first grapes from the vineyards and is ideal if you live near a wine-growing region. In the spirit of Bacchus, the Roman god of wine, decorate the room with sprays of vine, bunches of grapes and pottery jugs. Cast-iron platters with intricate detailing are the thing, and rustic terracotta tiles also make great serving platforms.

Barbecued duck and nectarine salata in wonton cups

Makes 20

200 g	(6½ oz) Shortcrust Pastry (see Master Recipe)
⅓ cup	mascarpone cheese
2	eggs
	salt and freshly ground black pepper
1	eschalot (shallot or pickling onion), finely diced
2 tbsp	olive oil
1 cup	enokitake (enoki) mushrooms
1 cup	oyster mushrooms, each torn into 3 pieces
1 cup	baby button mushrooms, cut into quarters
1	bunch lemon thyme, leaves only

Preheat the oven to 170°C (325°F, gas mark 3).

Roll out the pastry thinly on floured cling film and cut out 20 circles, 5 cm (2 in) in diameter.

Place the circles in small non-stick mini muffin trays.

Prick the base of each one with a fork and bake for 10 minutes. Remove from the oven and set aside.

Whisk together the mascarpone, eggs and seasonings.

Fry the eschalot in 1 tablespoon of the oil until translucent.

In the remaining oil, brown the mushroom varieties separately and very quickly on high heat so they do not release moisture and stew.

Set aside.

Combine the eschalot, lemon thyme leaves and mushrooms.

Place 2 teaspoons of the mascarpone custard in each pastry shell.

Top with the mushroom mixture.

Bake in the oven for 15 minutes. Serve warm.

Forest mushroom
and mascarpone
tarts

Makes 20

The duck

½ Chinese barbecued duck,
skinned and flesh finely sliced

2 tbsp hoisin sauce

2 tbsp plum sauce

½ bunch mint, chopped

½ bunch coriander (cilantro), chopped

5 green onions (spring onions or scallions), chopped

2 fresh nectarines, finely sliced

Coat the duck in the hoisin and plum sauces.

Mix together the herbs, shallots and nectarine.

Toss lightly, taking care not to mash the nectarine.

Add the duck shortly before serving. Toss lightly to combine.

The wonton cups

20 wonton wrappers

1 cup vegetable oil

30 ml (1 fl oz) ladle

Trim the wonton wrappers into 5 cm (2 in) squares and separate.

Heat the oil and wrap a wonton wrapper around the outside of the ladle cup.

Immerse the ladle in the oil until the wonton is lightly browned and crisp, giving it a bowl shape.

Drain on absorbent paper.

Repeat for each wonton cup.

Just before serving, place the duck mixture in the wonton cups.

Barbecued duck
and nectarine
salata in
wonton cups

Makes 20

1	yellow capsicum (pepper)
1	red capsicum (pepper)
20	mussels, washed, beards removed
1	serve Bouillon (see Master Recipe)
2 tbsp	butter
1	serve Provençal Crumbs (see Master Recipe)

Preheat the oven to 220°C (425°F, gas mark 7). Bake the capsicums whole, turning regularly until the skin blisters on all sides.

Remove the skin and the seeds.

Dice the capsicum to ½ cm (¼ in) pieces.

Poach the mussels in the bouillon until they open. Discard any mussles that do not open.

Remove one side of shell and discard.

Loosen the mussel from the other shell.

Melt the butter in a saucepan.

Add the crumbs and toast lightly, stirring constantly until browned and crisp.

Place 1 teaspoon of diced capsicum on top of each mussel and sprinkle with Provençal crumbs.

Serve hot or cold. If reheating, do so gently to avoid toughening the mussels.

Chef's Tip

Mussels prepared in this style are also delicious as part of an antipasto platter.

Mussels with roasted capsicum and Provençal crumbs

Makes 20

2 cups	self-raising (self-rising) flour
1 tsp	salt and pepper
2	eggs
½ cup	melted butter
½ cup	milk
½ cup	julienned sun-dried tomatoes
1	bunch oregano leaves, coarsely chopped
½	bunch flat-leaf (Italian) parsley leaves, coarsely chopped
½ cup	crumbled feta cheese
¼ cup	grated Parmesan cheese (do not use pre-packaged grated cheese)

Sun-dried tomato muffins

Preheat the oven to 220°C (425°F, gas mark 7).

Sift the flour, salt and pepper.

Make a well in the centre and add the eggs, butter and milk.

Gradually work into the flour. Do this quickly without over-stirring to avoid the glutens in the flour stretching and bubbles forming during cooking, making your muffins tough.

Fold in tomatoes, herbs and cheeses.

Place heaped tablespoons of the mixture in greased non-stick miniature muffin tins.

Bake in the oven for about 15 minutes or until brown and crispy on the outside.

Serve either hot or cold, but bake only on the day of serving.

Chef's Tip

Taste your sun-dried tomatoes before you buy if you can. Many sun-dried tomatoes are treated with sulphur and have a bitter aftertaste which transfers to the muffins. I usually have the muffins in the oven as guests arrive, to ensure a delicious baking aroma spreads throughout the house.

Although hibernation is a natural instinct in wintertime, it pays to battle the cold. It's a treat to invite friends over to a roaring fire, whether in the fireplace or a hot coal brazier in the garden or on the balcony.

In decorating for a winter party, go for a 'bed and breakfast' feel using country motifs. Displays are easily made from farmhouse wood and wire, or you could even collect pine cones, pebbles and leaves for a homemade sculpture.

Winter

Leek and olive bread and butter pudding

Perhaps the best thing about winter is that it's when people really enjoy their food. It's the season for comfort food, and that's the inspiration behind the following recipes. Glühwein aside, why not serve Moscow Mules? The frozen vodka mixed with fresh limes and ginger ale should get the blood flowing, and they'll be especially appropriate if everyone arrives in their best faux-fur muffs, hats and coats!

Pork, apple and chestnut pies

1 loaf olive and onion bread (available from specialty
bakeries), thinly sliced
2/3 cup olive tapenade
2 cups Leek Béchamel (see Master Recipe)
1 cup grated vintage cheddar cheese (do not use pre-
packaged grated cheese)
1/4 cup extra olive tapenade
Crispy Leeks (see Master Recipe)

Preheat the oven to 180ºC (350ºF, gas mark 4).
Cover the base of a 15 cm x 15 cm x 2 cm (6 in x 6 in x 3/4 in)
tray with a single layer of the olive bread.
Divide the tapenade into 4 equal amounts.
Coat the bread layer evenly with tapenade, followed by a layer
of béchamel, then cheese.
Repeat until you have 4 layers.
Bake in the oven for 25 minutes.
Cool, then cut into 2 cm (3/4 in) squares, trimming the sides
neatly first.
Reheat for 10 minutes on a baking tray in a 170ºC (325ºF,
gas mark 3) oven.
Place 1/2 teaspoon of extra tapenade in the centre of each
square and garnish with crispy leeks.

Chef's Tip

This recipe is best made the day before serving so the
cheese sets, thereby making it easier to cut into neat
squares.
Make two and freeze one.
These are excellent to take on a winter picnic, as they are
quite tasty when eaten cold. Just cut them slightly larger
for lunch size.

Leek and olive bread and butter pudding

Makes 20

1	small onion, finely diced
1	clove garlic, crushed
1 tbsp	oil
200 g	(6½ oz) lean pork, diced
⅓ cup	apple juice
2 cups	chicken or veal stock
2	bay leaves
1	bunch sage leaves, julienned
2	Granny Smith apples, finely diced
2 tbsp	dried chestnuts, soaked in water for 4 hours, then coarsely chopped
	salt and freshly ground black pepper
1 tbsp	potato flour (available from health-food stores)
2 tbsp	cold water
2	sheets ready-made puff pastry
	milk, for glazing

Pork, apple and chestnut pies

Fry the onion and garlic in the oil until opaque.

Add the meat, turning occasionally until the pork is sealed.

Stir in the apple juice and simmer until the mixture reduces by approximately half. This will intensify the flavour.

Pour in the stock, add the bay and sage leaves, and simmer for 1 hour or until meat is tender but not falling apart.

Take the meat out of the liquid and chop into ½ cm (¼ in) dice (so it fits into moulds easily).

Add the apple and chestnuts and simmer for a further 20 minutes.

Season with salt and pepper. To thicken, mix the potato flour and water in a cup until smooth, then drizzle in slowly while stirring.

Preheat the oven to 180°C (350°F, gas mark 4).

Roll out the pastry thinly, cut to size and press into non-stick muffin tins to create the casings. Fill the casings with the pork mixture (it's a lot easier with a less chunky filling).

Cut pastry pig shapes for the top, glaze with milk and place on top of the filling.

Bake for 20 minutes or until golden brown and the pork tops have risen slightly. Serve hot.

Chef's Tip

I always keep extra pastry and mixture (separately) in the freezer – it keeps well, saves twice the work, and means I always have substantial small food for any occasion with only a little final preparation involved.

Makes 20

The potato skins

20 chat (baby) potatoes
vegetable oil
salt and freshly ground black pepper

Preheat the oven to 200°C (400°F, gas mark 6).
Use a melon-baller to scoop out the centre of each potato, leaving a hollow shell.
Rub in some oil, salt and pepper and roast in the oven for 20 minutes or until cooked through (test with a skewer – if it goes in easily, the potatoes are cooked).

The taramasalata

4 slices white bread, crusts removed
6 tbsp milk
350 g (11 oz) smoked, undyed cod's roe, skin on
½ red onion, diced
juice of 1 lemon
1 garlic clove, crushed
freshly ground black pepper
½ tsp wasabi paste
⅓ cup extra virgin olive oil
2 tbsp orange flying-fish roe, to garnish
2 tbsp blond flying-fish roe, to garnish

Dice the bread and place in a bowl with the milk to soften.
Cut open the skin of the cod's roe and scrape the eggs into a food processor. Process for 30 seconds.
Add the red onion, lemon juice, garlic, pepper and wasabi and process to combine.
With the machine running, add the olive oil in a steady stream until the consistency is quite thick.
Test for seasoning and add a little more lemon juice if there is a slight aftertaste or if it is slightly bland. Scrape the sides and process again.
To serve, fill the potato skins with 1 heaped tablespoon of the taramasalata and garnish with the flying-fish roes.

Chef's Tip

The taramasalata is also delicious as a dip.

Potato skins with blond taramasalata and flying-fish roe

Makes 20

¼ Japanese pumpkin (Japanese/kabocha squash),
peeled and seeds removed
olive oil spray
Lime Leaf Chicken (see Master Recipe)

Preheat the oven to 170°C (325°F, gas mark 3).
Cut the pumpkin into 2 cm (¾ in) squares.
Using a melon-baller, make a well in the centre deep enough for filling but still leaving the sides sturdy.
Spray with oil and bake for 15 minutes or until just starting to soften.
Fill the pumpkin casings with the Lime Leaf Chicken.

Chef's Tip

There will be a fair amount of wastage when you trim a round pumpkin into squares but leftovers can be used the next day in a stir-fry or soup.

Roast pumpkin squares with lime leaf chicken

A sense of occasion makes the difference between a party and a gathering. The food, drink and guest list are all essential, but it's that indefinable something in the air that binds the rest together. And it doesn't create itself. No matter how bubbly the people you've invited, always put some thought into how you can set the template for a mood of celebration.

The venue and type of event are the starting points, marking the parameters within which you can work your magic. See what you can do to decorate the space, and do so in a way that serves your theme. Then there's the actual occasion.

Occasions
Any excuse is a good excuse for a party ...

A birthday is always the perfect excuse for a party and knows no bounds of enjoyment, whether casual, formal, exotic or amusingly themed, for a child, a senior or even a favourite pet. Baby's naming day will likely be a gentle affair, decked out in pink or blue, while high spirits will prevail at a birthday barbecue.

Other occasions tend to be more specific in focus and theme. For situations such as weddings and Christmas, you'll want to go the whole hog in decorating (flowers and embarrassing photographs for the former, fairy lights and bunting for the latter). Others, such as a open-air concert in the park, lend themselves to picnics, while a party with the guys in honour of a sporting final is likely to be a more casual, even rowdy, affair. And Valentine's Day is the perfect time to organise an intimate surprise breakfast for that special person in your life. Who knows, if you do it well, you might well be in the running for a wedding party of your own!

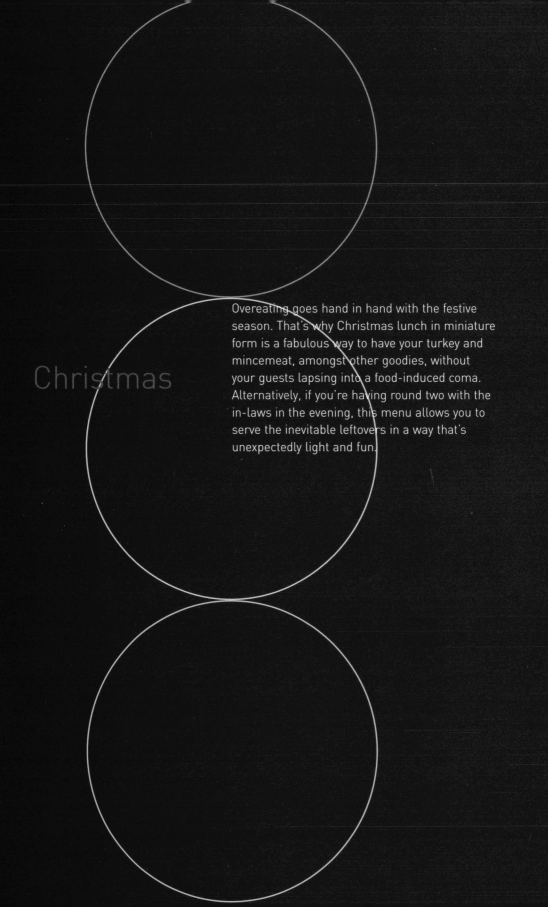

Christmas

Overeating goes hand in hand with the festive season. That's why Christmas lunch in miniature form is a fabulous way to have your turkey and mincemeat, amongst other goodies, without your guests lapsing into a food-induced coma. Alternatively, if you're having round two with the in-laws in the evening, this menu allows you to serve the inevitable leftovers in a way that's unexpectedly light and fun.

Oysters with Champagne sabayon

To serve these morsels, decorate the edges of simple glass platters with a little holly. If setting the platters on a table, use a woven seasonal wreath as a base. As for Christmas cheer, how about vodka or Champagne mixed with cranberry juice? It's very easy and very festive. A Brandy Alexander is another ideal Christmas cocktail, and makes a nice change when served with traditional mince pies instead of the usual brandy butter.

Miniature Christmas dinner

Makes 20

¼ bottle Champagne
(or good-quality sparkling white wine)
6 egg yolks
1 tbsp lemon juice
1 tbsp raspberry vinegar
salt to taste
20 ocean-bred oysters, such as Pacific or
Japanese oysters

Place the Champagne, egg yolks, lemon juice, raspberry
vinegar and salt in a double boiler.
Whisk constantly over boiling water for about 15 minutes or
until thick and fluffy.
Spoon over the oysters.
Serve oysters with forks or skewered on toothpicks.

Chef's Tip

The ocean-bred variety of oysters is better for this recipe
as the flavour is more subtle than the river varieties.

Oysters with Champagne sabayon

Makes 20

1 cup	peeled and sliced pumpkin pieces
5	small Brussels sprouts
20	slices of brioche loaf, ½ cm x 7 cm x 7 cm (¼ in x 2¾ in x 2¾ in) each, crusts removed
2 tbsp	melted butter
5	small cherry tomatoes, cut into quarters
150 g	(5 oz) cooked turkey breast, cut into 20 slices
	salt and freshly ground black pepper
2 tbsp	Provençal Crumbs (see Master Recipe)
4	tbsp cranberry sauce

Preheat the oven to 180°C (350°F, gas mark 4).

Bake the pumpkin until cooked but still firm.

Boil the Brussels sprouts until cooked but still firm and green. Cool and cut into quarters.

Brush the brioche slices with butter and press into 5 cm (2 in) tartlet moulds.

Bake in a 180°C (350°F, gas mark 4) oven until golden brown.

Arrange the cherry tomatoes, pumpkin slices, Brussels sprouts and turkey slices in the tartlet cases and season.

Heat for about 5 minutes at 150°C (300°F, gas mark 2).

To serve, remove from the oven and top with a light sprinkling of the Provençal crumbs and 1 teaspoon of the cranberry sauce.

Miniature
Christmas dinner

Chef's Tip

Make all the components the day before, and simply compile them just before serving.

Makes 20

The brandy butter

4 tbsp unsalted butter at room temperature
2 tbsp icing (confectioners') sugar
1 tbsp brandy

Blend all ingredients together in a food processor until combined, about 1 minute.

The crackers

8 sheets filo (phyllo) pastry
2 tbsp melted butter
2 cups good-quality fruit mince
       icing (confectioners') sugar, for dusting
       holly sprigs or red currants, to garnish

Preheat the oven to 220°C (425°F, gas mark 7).
Lay 1 sheet of filo on a board and brush with butter.
Lay another sheet of filo on top and butter it too.
Cut the sheets evenly into 8 rectangles, cutting 4 panels across, then 4 horizontally.
Repeat with the remaining filo.
Take 1 rectangle and place a sausage of fruit mince on it lengthwise.
Make an indent in the sausage and fill with 1 teaspoon of the brandy butter.
Roll up and gently twist both ends.
Finish the rest of the crackers in the same manner.
Transfer the crackers to an oiled baking tray.
Hold open the ends with little balls of foil.
Bake in the oven for 10 minutes.
Dust with icing sugar and garnish with the holly or red currants.

Mincemeat crackers with brandy butter

Chef's Tip

For fun you could put little ovenproof prizes in the centre. (Make sure you tell your guests – you don't want anyone to chip a tooth!)
Always keep the filo covered with a damp tea towel (kitchen towel) during preparation or it will dry out.
For a neat effect, use crimping scissors to shape the edges before you roll the pastry.

Makes 20

10 eggs
2 tbsp milk
salt and freshly ground black pepper
⅓ cup crème fraîche (or light sour cream)
4 sprigs of dill, stalks removed, leaves finely chopped
small bunch of chives, finely chopped
zest of ½ lemon
15 slices smoked salmon

Beat together the eggs, milk, salt and pepper.
Make 5 omelettes, each time pouring the egg mixture thinly and evenly over the base of a greased frying pan on medium heat. When set, remove the omelettes from the pan and set aside.
Combine the crème fraîche, dill, chives and zest.
Spread the crème fraîche mixture evenly over the omelettes.
Arrange 3 slices of salmon on each omelette and roll up tightly.
Refrigerate, then slice evenly into 20 rolls, each 2 cm (3/4 in) in size.
Serve with the cut side facing up like a pinwheel.

Chef's Tip

This recipe can be made the day before serving and stored in an airtight container in the refrigerator. Bring back to room temperature before serving.

Omelette and
smoked salmon
rolls

Modern weddings tend to be less formal and less strictly organised than those of past generations. While the post-nuptial bash will still be elegant, there's often less emphasis on hugely involved and expensive receptions. Practice today leans more towards the stand-up cocktail party, and there are lots of good reasons to take this option. Contemporary couples are more often paying for their weddings themselves; they may be tying the knot for a second or more time; or they may simply prefer to celebrate in a simpler, low-fuss fashion.

Guests, however, never change. They still expect to be fed. Even at an afternoon reception, many people will have skipped lunch in anticipation. So when small-and-

Weddings

Lemon and nutmeg potted crab with Parmesan and chive palmiers (left)
Sun-dried tomato and rosemary biscotti with beef carpaccio (right)

dainty food is the order of the day, be prepared and have plenty of it. A great way of satisfying even the traditionalists is to turn the reception into a progressive dinner. Organise entrée-style canapés (perhaps three different types), four choices of more robust main course-style items, and finish with petits fours-style desserts.

Beverages follow suit: cocktails and a good Champagne on arrival, a hearty red and white wine for the main, a Sauternes or muscat with dessert, and finally coffee with the wedding cake.

Makes 20

The lemon and nutmeg potted crab

	zest of 1 lemon
2 cups	cooked crab meat
	pinch Maldon (kosher) sea salt and freshly ground black pepper
250 g	(8 oz) butter
¼ tsp	nutmeg

Add half the lemon zest to the crab, then add salt and pepper.
Pack the crab into ramekins.
Heat the butter with the remaining lemon zest and the nutmeg.
Pour the clear butter off the residue and set aside. Use this butter to pour over the crab, then refrigerate until set.

The Parmesan and chive palmiers

1	sheet ready-made puff pastry
2 tbsp	grated Parmesan cheese (do not use pre-packaged grated cheese)
2 tbsp	chopped chives

Preheat the oven to 200°C (400°F, gas mark 6).
Cut the sheet of pastry into a 10 cm x 20 cm (4 in x 8 in) rectangle.
Sprinkle on the Parmesan cheese and chives.
Tightly roll one long side into the middle, then roll the opposite long side into the middle. It should resemble an upper-case 'B' lying on its back.
Cut the roll into 1 cm (⅓ in) slices.
Press each slice with your fingertips until it is ½ cm (¼ in) high but retains its shape.
Place the palmiers on a baking tray. Grease the base of another baking tray, then place it on top of the palmiers to prevent excessive rising.
Bake in the oven for 20 minutes or until crisp.
Cool, then seal in an airtight container.
To assemble, place the potted crab meat on the palmiers.

Chef's Tip

Potted crab will keep in the refrigerator for up to three days. The palmiers will keep for a week in an airtight container. You can also use prawns (shrimp) in place of the crab.

Lemon and nutmeg potted crab with Parmesan and chive palmiers

Makes 20

The tomato and rosemary biscotti

1²/₃	cups whole blanched almonds
2 tbsp	fresh rosemary leaves
1 cup	plain (all-purpose) flour
½ cup	cornflour (cornstarch)
½ tsp	baking powder
2	eggs
2 tbsp	sun-dried tomatoes, julienned

Preheat the oven to 180ºC (350ºF, gas mark 4).

Place the almonds and rosemary in the bowl of a food processor and process finely.

Add the two flours, the baking powder and the eggs and process until incorporated.

Remove from bowl and knead in the sun-dried tomatoes. If the mixture seems slightly crumbly, add a few drops of water until it becomes a dough with a smooth, silken texture.

Roll the dough into a log and place on a greased baking tray.

Bake in the oven for 20 minutes, then remove. Reduce the oven temperature to 120°C (250ºF, gas mark ½).

Slice the log into rounds ½ cm (¼ in) wide and lay flat on the baking tray. Return the tray to the oven.

Bake again for 5–10 minutes or until crisp.

The carpaccio

200 g	(6½ oz) beef fillet
2 tbsp	Salsa Verde (see Master Recipe)

Remove the sinews and fat from the beef.

Roll the fillet in the salsa verde.

Wrap tightly in cling film so that it resembles a sausage.

Freeze for 30 minutes.

Remove from the freezer and immediately cut the fillet into wafer-thin slices.

Place curled beef slices on the biscotti.

Serve when the beef comes to room temperature.

Chef's Tip

Freezing the beef for this short amount of time makes slicing into wafers much easier – and the slices will be more even.

Sun-dried tomato and rosemary biscotti with beef carpaccio

Makes 20

The shells

200 g (6½ oz) Shortcrust Pastry (see Master Recipe)

Preheat the oven to 140°C (275°F, gas mark 1).
Roll the pastry very thin between layers of cling film.
Cut 20 circles, each 4 cm (1½ in) in diameter.
Place on mini madeleine trays and mould into scallop shells.
Bake in the oven for 25 minutes.

The coquilles

20 small sea scallops
1 tsp butter
2 tbsp lemon thyme leaves
2 tbsp Mayonnaise (see Master Recipe)

Clean and trim the sinew from the scallops.
In a frying pan, fry the scallops in the butter for 1 minute with half
the lemon thyme leaves.
Remove from the pan.
Turn the scallops through the mayonnaise to give them a light
coating.
Place the scallops on the pastry shells and serve immediately.

Chef's Tip

The shells can be made up to two days in advance if kept in an
airtight container in the refrigerator. Reheat before serving.

Coquilles St
Jacques in
shell pastries

Makes 20

The tarts

100 g (3½ oz) fresh angel-hair saffron pasta
1 egg white
pinch of rock salt
pinch of ground pepper

Preheat the oven to 160ºC (325ºF, gas mark 3).
Mix all the ingredients together.
Take three or four strands of the pasta and press into a greased non-stick mini muffin mould, making sure that the base is properly covered but that there is still a good-size well in the centre.
Bake for 10 minutes in the oven. Cool and set aside.

The truffle custard

2 eschalots (shallots or pickling onions), finely chopped
1 tbsp olive oil
1 cup enokitake (enoki) mushrooms
2 tbsp lemon thyme leaves
⅓ cup dry white wine
1⅓ cups pouring (single) cream
1 small black truffle, finely shaved on a Chinese mandoline slicer
3 eggs, beaten
salt and freshly ground black pepper

Saffron noodle tarts with truffle custard and enokitake mushrooms

Pan-fry the eschalots in the oil until opaque, then add half the enokitake mushrooms. Add in the lemon thyme leaves and white wine. Simmer the mixture until reduced by two-thirds.
Pour in the cream, continue to simmer and reduce by half.
Add the truffle, remove from the heat and allow to cool.
Stir in beaten eggs and season with salt and pepper.
Preheat the oven to 150ºC (300ºF, gas mark 2).
Place 1 teaspoon of the mixture in the non-stick muffin pans.
Bake for 15 minutes or until the mixture is firm to the touch.
Deep-fry the remaining enokitake mushrooms until crisp, then drain on absorbent paper.
To serve, turn out the custards into the noodle cases and top with the fried enokitake mushrooms.

Chef's Tip

When cooking custard or egg in an oven, do so on a slow heat or the mixture will bubble, loose its creamy texture and become rubbery.

Baby's naming day

I have themed this section around little boys and their special colour. It's a natural bias – I have a little boy whose christening day we celebrated in the best spirit of baby blue. Bouncing boys are one thing, but when it comes to little girls, even more fuss tends to be made over them. Last year, for instance, I catered for a gorgeous all-pink party.

Miniature blueberry tarts

For Benjamin's bash we decorated the venue with white and blue bells, blue balloons and flower arrangements of lilies. He was born in the Chinese Year of the Rabbit, so bunnies were incorporated into the theme as well. We served the food on country-style wooden trays and in Benjamin Bunny baskets adorned with blue ribbons. The afternoon rounded up with a good cup of tea and a slice of baby-blue rocking-horse cake.

As for drinks, at these occasions it's probably best to go low key, perhaps some Champagne, a punch, or gin and tonics if you dare. After all, you are meant to set an example for the youngsters!

Rabbit and olive pies

Makes 20

The tart shells
½ quantity of Sweet Shortcrust Pastry
(see Master Recipe)

Preheat the oven to 170ºC (325ºF, gas mark 3).
Roll out the pastry thinly on floured cling film and cut out 20 circles, 5 cm (2 in) in diameter.
Place the circles in small non-stick mini muffin trays.
Prick the base of each one with a fork and bake for 10 minutes.

The filling
⅓ cup dry white wine
4 egg yolks
⅓ cup sugar
1 tbsp gelatin powder
2 tbsp cold water
1 punnet blueberries
icing (confectioners') sugar, to garnish

Whisk the wine, egg yolks and sugar to a thick consistency in a double-boiler over boiling water. This will take about 15 minutes of constant whisking.
Soak the gelatin in the water, then dissolve it in the microwave for 1 minute on High.
Whisk in the warm gelatin.
Spoon the filling into the tarts to about two-thirds full, then arrange the blueberries on top.
To finish, sprinkle with a little icing sugar.

Chef's Tip

If your arm gets tired in the whisking process, take the filling off the heat until you can continue, otherwise the mixture will curdle.
You can make your filling mixture separately the day before but fill the tarts only on the day of the party or the pastry will loose its crispness.

Miniature
blueberry tarts

Makes 20

1	small onion, chopped
1	clove garlic, chopped
1	bay leaf
1 tsp	fresh sage, chopped
1 tsp	fresh lemon thyme, chopped
1 tbsp	vegetable oil
1	rabbit, quartered
1 tbsp	olive tapenade
½ cup	dry white wine
2 cups	chicken stock
2 tbsp	potato flour (available from health-food stores)
2 tbsp	cold water
3	sheets ready-made puff pastry
20	good quality olives, pitted and sliced
	milk, for glazing

Rabbit and olive pies

In a large saucepan, fry the onion, garlic, bay leaf, sage and lemon thyme in the oil until soft.

Add the rabbit, tapenade, wine and stock.

Simmer the casserole slowly for 1 hour or until the rabbit is tender. Set aside to cool.

Mix the potato flour in the water and add to the casserole to thicken the sauce.

Remove the rabbit meat and shred. Return the meat to the mixture.

Preheat the oven to 180°C (350°F, gas mark 4).

Cut 20 circles, 5 cm (2 in) in diameter, from the puff pastry and line small tartlet pans with the pastry circles.

Fill the casings with the rabbit mixture and sliced olives.

Cut out 20 rabbit shapes from the puff pastry with a pastry cutter and place them on top of the pies.

Brush with milk and bake for 15 minutes or until golden brown.

Serve hot.

Chef's Tip

Make the pies the day before using. The rabbit mixture is fine to freeze, so you can make it in advance or prepare double the amount for next time.

Makes 20

1	medium-sized rainbow trout, skinned, boned and cut into small slices, each 2 cm (3/4 in) long and 1/2 cm (1/4 in) thick
3 tbsp	caster (superfine) sugar
1 tbsp	Maldon (kosher) sea salt
1/4 tsp	freshly ground black pepper
4	sprigs of dill, leaves only, finely chopped
20	Potato Galettes (see Master Recipe)
2 tbsp	crème fraîche (or light sour cream)
1	bunch chives

Mix trout slices with sugar, salt, pepper and dill.

Marinate for 1 hour, then pour off the accumulated juices.

Fill each galette with 3 slices of trout and top with dab of crème fraîche.

Serve garnished with long straws of chives.

Chef's Tip

The salt and sugar act as a curing agent for the trout. The mixture can be kept for up to one week in the refrigerator, provided the liquid is poured off regularly.

Potato galettes
with sugar-cured
trout

Makes 20

1 cup	sugar
1 cup	treacle or molasses
1 cup	vegetable oil
3	eggs, lightly beaten
1 cup	boiling water
1 tsp	salt
1 tsp	ground cloves
1 tsp	ground ginger
1 tsp	ground cinnamon
2 cups	plain (all-purpose) flour
2 tsp	baking soda
2/3 cup	chopped white chocolate
2 tbsp	pouring (single) cream

Preheat the oven to 180ºC (350ºF, gas mark 4).

Mix together the sugar, treacle or molasses, oil and eggs.

Add the boiling water and mix thoroughly.

Sieve the dry ingredients together and combine with the molasses mixture.

Pour into a non-stick loaf tin.

Bake in the oven for 1½ hours.

Cool and slice.

Use a gingerbread man shaped cutter to cut out two men per slice.

Melt together the white chocolate and cream for 1 minute in the microwave on Medium, stirring until combined.

Transfer the chocolate mixture to a piping bag and pipe on the face and buttons.

Baby gingerbread men

Chef's Tip

Gingerbread is better made the day before cutting, as it tends to crumble if you slice it fresh.

Most large cities have a fabulous central park which in summer plays host to a variety of outdoor entertainment. Whether it's opera, a symphony concert or a play by Shakespeare, taking a picnic is an enjoyable, civilised way to wait for the show to begin as you lay claim to the best position in the park by arriving early. Everything in your basketed feast needs to be easy to handle, and a French Champagne or premium sparkling wine is the best thing to quaff.

An open-air concert in the park

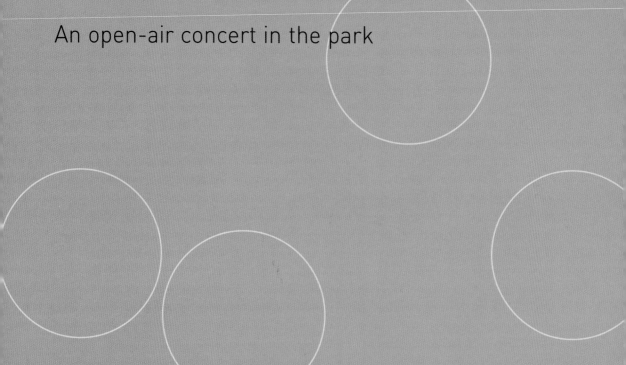

Individual tuna Niçoise salads

Muffletta

Makes 20

10 medium-sized potatoes
vegetable oil, for basting
salt and freshly ground black pepper
⅓ cup Salsa Verde (see Master Recipe)
200 g (6½ oz) piece of tuna
20 long French beans (haricot verts), cut into three equal lengths and blanched
20 baby olives
10 yellow teardrop tomatoes, cut in half
10 cherry tomatoes, cut in half
10 quail eggs, boiled, shelled and cut in half
20 anchovies (traditional, but optional)

Individual tuna Niçoise salads

Preheat the oven to 200ºC (400ºF, gas mark 6).

Cut the potatoes in half and use a melon-baller to scoop out the centre from each.

Rub the hollowed-out potatoes and the centre pieces with oil, salt and pepper.

Roast all the potatoes in the oven for 20 minutes or until cooked through.

Rub a small amount of the salsa verde on the tuna, then char-grill on all sides, leaving the centre rare.

Cool and then dice the tuna.

Coat the tuna and potato centres with a small amount of salsa verde.

Mix the beans, olives, tomatoes, eggs and anchovies together then mix all with the tuna and potato centres.

To serve, fill the potato skins with the tuna mixture.

Chef's Tip

To stop the potatoes from sliding about, cut a small flat slice from each base.

When roasting potatoes to later serve cold, always roast on the day of serving and to a little more crisp than usual.

Makes 20

1	good-quality, French-style baguette
1	eggplant (aubergine)
2	zucchinis (courgettes)
2 tbsp	olive oil
	salt and freshly ground black pepper
30	slices Danish (or mild) salami
½	bunch of basil, leaves only
⅓ cup	grated vintage cheddar cheese (do not use pre-packaged grated cheese)
1	red capsicum (pepper), roasted, skinned, seeds removed

Preheat the oven to 200ºC (400ºF, gas mark 6).

Slice a thin layer off the top of the baguette, leaving one side joined.

Pull out the soft centre of the bread and discard.

Slice the eggplant and zucchini lengthwise.

Rub with the oil, salt and pepper and roast in the oven until soft.

Fill the bread with layers of salami, basil leaves, cheese, eggplant, capsicum and zucchini.

Replace the top of the bread.

Wrap in foil and bake in the oven at 200°C for 15 minutes.

Cool, then cut into 20 slices.

Chef's Tip

These can be prepared the day before and baked on the day. Keep the roast capsicum separate until cooking as its moisture will saturate the bread if added too far in advance.

Muffletta

Makes 20

The lime mayonnaise

⅓ cup	Mayonnaise (see Master Recipe)
1	drop of lime oil
	(available from gourmet food stores)
	zest of 1 lime

Mix all the lime mayonnaise ingredients together in a bowl.

The lobster

1	cooked lobster or crayfish,
	weighing approximately 1 kg (2 lb)
1	butter lettuce
1	mignonette lettuce
1	good-quality sourdough baguette, cut into 40 thin slices
	Lime Mayonnaise
1	small bunch chervil

Miniature lobster sandwiches with lime mayonnaise

Slice the lobster meat thinly.

Place mixed lettuce leaves on 20 slices of the bread.

Top with a slice of lobster.

Garnish with 1 teaspoon of the lime mayonnaise and a sprig of chervil.

Top with a slice of bread and serve.

Chef's Tip

If the sandwiches have to sit for a long time, it's best to wrap them individually in greaseproof paper.

If you can't find butter or mignonette lettuce, substitute two non-bitter varieties with interesting colours and leaf shapes.

Makes 20

200 g	(6½ oz) Sweet Shortcrust Pastry (see Master Recipe)
2 tbsp	almond meal, dry-roasted
2 tbsp	sliced almonds, dry-roasted, skin left on
½ cup	crème fraîche (or light sour cream)
1 cup	mascarpone cheese
¼ cup	icing (confectioners') sugar seeds of ½ vanilla bean
1	punnet strawberries

Preheat the oven to 180ºC (350ºF, gas mark 4).

Sprinkle almond meal over a piece of plastic wrap or cling film.

Place the pastry on top and place another sheet of plastic wrap over that. Roll until very thin.

Place 20 oiled 5 cm (2 in) square tins on a baking sheet and place the almond pastry on top.

Roll over with a rolling pin to remove excess dough.

Lightly press 2 or 3 of the almond slices into each square.

Bake for 15–20 minutes or until golden brown.

Process the crème fraîche, mascarpone, icing sugar and the vanilla seeds for 30 seconds.

Remove shortcakes from tins.

Place 1 heaped teaspoon of cream in the middle and top with strawberries.

Chef's Tip

Prick the base of the pastry to stop bubbles forming during cooking.

Baby strawberry shortcake

Birthday barbecue

If it's your birthday you'll want to enjoy yourself with the minimum of fuss. Seafood and meat items that can be barbecued without much adornment are easiest to manage. If you just let the produce speak for itself and stay out of the kitchen, you'll have much more time for really important things, such as opening presents and having a drink or two with your friends.

Vodka jelly shots are fantastic party starters. Just follow the directions on the back of the gelatine packet for the liquid ratio. My favourite combination is vodka with cranberry juice. Set them in little plastic shot glasses and hand them out as people arrive. Your guests will be in a party mood in no time at all!

Skewers of salmon and dill (foreground) and Roast asparagus wrapped in proscuitto

Makes 20

20 asparagus spears
10 slices prosciutto (parma ham),
     sliced in half lengthwise
     extra virgin olive oil
     Maldon (kosher) sea salt and
     freshly ground black pepper

Using a sharp knife, cut the bottom ends off the asparagus spears diagonally.
Coil the prosciutto vertically around the asparagus stem.
Drizzle the olive oil over the top of the asparagus and sprinkle with the seasonings.
Barbecue for 5 minutes on the plate section (not the perforated grill), turning once.

Chef's Tip

Use medium-sized asparagus. If they're too large, the prosciutto will be overcooked before the asparagus is cooked through; too small and the heat will shrivel the tips.

Roast asparagus
wrapped in
prosciutto

Makes 20

750 g (1 lb 8 oz) salmon fillet,
    skinned and bones removed
20 bamboo skewers, soaked in water for 30 minutes

The pistou

2 large garlic cloves
    zest of ½ lemon
1 cup pistachio nuts, shelled and dry-roasted
2 large bunches dill
12 chive stalks
1 bunch flat-leaf (Italian) parsley
    salt, to taste
1 cup extra virgin olive oil

Skewers of
salmon and dill
with pistachio
pistou

Cut the salmon into 2 cm (¾ in) cubes, then thread onto the skewers.

Place the garlic and the lemon zest in a food processor and chop coarsely.

Add the pistachios and process for 50 seconds.

With the motor running, add the dill, chives, parsley and salt.

Set the machine to low and add the olive oil in a steady thin stream. When fully blended, transfer the mixture to a bowl.

Roll the salmon cubes in the pistou, then cook on the barbecue for 45 seconds each side.

Chef's Tip

Soaking the skewers in water for 30 minutes prior to cooking reduces the risk of burning the wood or bamboo.

Makes 20

 20 scallops in the shells
½ cup chopped, unsalted butter
     juice and zest of 1 lemon
     pinch of salt
 20 sprigs of lemon thyme, leaves only

Remove the scallops from the shells and slice off any excess sinew. Clean, leaving the roe intact.
Return the scallops to the shells.
Blend the butter, lemon juice, zest, salt and lemon thyme in a food processor.
Transfer to a sheet of cooking foil and wrap into a log shape, then store in the refrigerator.
When the lemon butter has solidified, cut into 20 slices.
Place the lemon-butter slices on the scallops. Barbecue the scallops in their shells for 1 minute on each side, turning them in their shells.
Serve immediately.

Scallops grilled in
the shell with
lemon thyme

Chef's Tip
   Choose nice plump scallops that are firm to the touch.

Makes 20

5	baby racks of lamb, four cutlets on each
	salt
4 tsp	ground cumin
2 tsp	ground black pepper
2 tsp	harissa or minced chillies
1 tsp	ground coriander seeds
1 tbsp	fresh oregano
2	cloves garlic
	grated zest of 2 lemons
	juice of 1 lemon
½ cup	extra virgin olive oil

Marinated baby lamb cutlets

Trim the baby lamb racks of excess fat and sinew.

Season the lamb with salt.

Combine all the remaining ingredients in a large shallow bowl to form the marinade, then add the lamb.

Rub the mixture into the flesh and leave to marinate for 2–3 hours, turning occasionally.

Cook the lamb racks on the barbecue for 5 minutes on each side.

Baste with the marinade, then leave to rest for 15 minutes before carving into individual cutlets.

Chef's Tip

Cook for 5 minutes each side as a guide for pink lamb. Cook longer if the racks are larger. Unlike beef, lamb is better served medium rare because of its higher fat content.

Resting is essential for cooked meats to retain their juices and tenderness. If you are worried about the lamb cooling, return to the heat for a couple of minutes after the resting process.

Valentine's Day breakfast for two

A menu designed to feed 20 would be rather strange in the context of Valentine's Day. Therefore, the following recipes make quantities for just two people, though there will probably be enough in the way of leftovers to last you both for a few romance-filled days. A word of advice: do whatever preparation you can the day before, and if you really want to pamper the object of your affections, not to mention yourself, consider hiring someone to serve the breakfast.

Hash brown tartlets with smoked salmon and poached quail egg

Remember, surprise and spontaneity are worth trying for on Valentine's Day. They really do ensure maximum thematic, and dramatic, effect. Once, for instance, I suggested to an old flame that we take a walk on a lonely cliff top prior to our dinner engagement. Lo and behold, as we rounded the corner we were met by a waiter sporting French Champagne and caviar blinis on a silver tray, with further goodies on a candlelit table. I had pre-plated the three courses, so all the waiter had to do was serve. When we disappeared into the sunset, he took it all away again.

Roses are the flowers to choose when decorating the table for this breakfast, complementing as they do crisp linen napkins and orange juice served in wine glasses. The adventurous might also like to indulge in an espresso martini: put a couple of shots of good, fresh, strong coffee, with a similar amount of vodka, in a cocktail shaker with ice and shake vigorously, then pour into martini glasses and sprinkle with chocolate powder.

Blueberry pancakes with mango and passionfruit butter

Serves 2

The hash browns

1 large potato, grated
   salt and freshly ground black pepper
1 green onion (spring onion or scallion), finely sliced
   butter

Preheat the oven to 220ºC (425ºF, gas mark 7).
Mix potatoes, seasoning and green onion together in a bowl.
Grease 2 round-based 5 cm (2 in) diameter tartlet tins with plenty of butter.
Press the potato mixture into the tins.
Bake in the oven for 15 minutes or until golden brown.

The salmon

2 quail eggs
2 slices smoked salmon
2 tbsp Hollandaise Sauce (see Master Recipe)
2 tsp salmon roe
2 chives

Poach the quail eggs in simmering water for 90 seconds, remove from the water and set aside until needed.
Construct by placing a slice of salmon on top of the hash brown and then add the egg.
Drizzle the hollandaise sauce over.
Spoon on the roe and garnish with chives.

Chef's Tip

To prepare ahead, poach the eggs, immerse in cold water immediately and leave overnight. Drain thoroughly before using.

Hash brown
tartlets with
smoked salmon
and poached
quail egg

Serves 2

The pancakes

1 cup	plain (all-purpose) flour
1	egg, beaten
1 tbsp	melted butter
½ cup	milk
	pinch of salt
	pinch of nutmeg
⅔ cup	blueberries

Process all the ingredients except the blueberries to a smooth but liquid batter. If the mixture is too thick, add a little more milk.

Pour one-quarter of the batter onto a hot, greased skillet or pan.

Sprinkle blueberries onto the pancake. When the base is brown and bubbles form on the top, flip it over to cook the other side.

Use a knife to test that the centre is cooked, then remove from pan and keep warm.

Repeat with the remaining batter and blueberries.

The butter

2 tbsp	icing (confectioners') sugar
½ cup	chopped butter at room temperature
1	medium-sized ripe mango
2	passionfruit

In a food processor, blend the sugar, butter, the flesh of half the mango and the pulp of 1 passionfruit for 30 seconds.

Place the mixture on a sheet of foil, shape it into a roll, then refrigerate for 30 minutes.

When the mixture has hardened, slice it into 4 equal disks.

To serve, slice the other half of the mango and layer with the hot pancakes and butter disks.

Top with more blueberries and the pulp of the remaining passionfruit.

Dust with icing sugar before serving.

Chef's Tip

Use a heavy-based frying pan or skillet. For best results keep the pan at medium heat. If the pan is too hot, the base of the pancake will burn before the mixture has cooked through.

Blueberry pancakes with mango and passionfruit butter

Serves 2

2 egg (plum) tomatoes, cut in half lengthwise
salt and freshly ground black pepper
6 potatoes, cut into ½ cm (¼ in) slices,
then into heart shapes
1 tbsp olive oil
1 avocado, flesh sliced thinly
2 large slices leg ham, coarsely chopped
2 tbsp Salsa Verde (see Master Recipe)

Season the cut side of each tomato with salt and pepper.
Grill the tomatoes until brown and cooked through.
Pan-fry the potato hearts in the oil until cooked.
Place a heart on each plate, then layer with avocado, tomato and ham, then another heart.
Press down firmly to stabilise the structure.
Repeat the layering process, again pressing down firmly on the top potato.
Drizzle with salsa verde and serve.

Chef's Tip

All items can be prepared a day in advance except for the slicing of the avocado as it will go brown. Reheat the cooked items for 10 minutes in a hot oven before assembling.

Heart-shaped hot potato and ham stacks

Serves 2

1	chorizo sausage (Spanish or Mexican)
1 tsp	olive oil
6	slices white bread, cut into halves
¼ cup	flat-leaf (Italian) parsley leaves
¼ cup	chopped chives
¼ cup	basil leaves
60 g	(2 oz) cheddar cheese, cut into thin slices
3	eggs
½ cup	pouring (single) cream
⅓ cup	Tomato Sauce (see Master Recipe)

Preheat the oven to 170°C (325°C, gas mark 3).

Slice the chorizo sausage thinly lengthwise, then pan-fry in the oil until brown on both sides.

Layer a 6 cm x 12 cm (2½ in x 4¾ in) loaf tin with alternate layers of bread, chorizo, herbs and cheddar, starting and finishing with a slice of bread.

Whisk together the eggs and the cream.

Pour into the loaf tin, soaking the bread all the way through.

Place the tin in the oven and bake for 25 minutes.

Remove from oven and allow to cool for at least 2 hours.

Slice thickly, then pan-fry until brown on both sides.

Serve with the tomato sauce and your choice of herb leaves as a garnish.

Feather-bed eggs

Chef's Tip

Making the loaf the day before serving will give the egg mixture more time to set, making slicing a lot easier.

Gatherings in honour of sports events are usually excitable, rowdy affairs, heavily peppered with elation if your team wins and misery if it doesn't.

Whatever sport you follow, there is likely to be plenty of testosterone pervading the ether on the big night. That's why I've based this menu around meat and potatoes. Yes, the idea is to soak up the beer, and while these recipes are indeed tasty, they shouldn't prove too much of a distraction from the main point of the evening. Until half-time, that is.

Sports night with the guys

Beef and burgundy pies (left)
Potato skins with bacon, sour cream and chives (right)

Makes 20

500 g	(1 lb) lean stewing beef, very thinly diced
2 tbsp	vegetable oil
1	onion, sliced
1	clove garlic, chopped
1½	cups red burgundy (or shiraz)
4	bay leaves
1½ cups	beef stock
2 cups	miniature button mushrooms, cut into quarters
2 tbsp	potato flour (available from health-food stores)
2 tbsp	cold water
3	sheets ready-made puff pastry
1	egg yolk

In a saucepan, seal the beef in batches in some of the oil. Set aside until needed.

Add the onion and the garlic to the saucepan with a little more oil and fry until opaque.

Return the beef to the saucepan, pour in two-thirds of the wine and add the bay leaves.

Simmer to reduce the liquid by one-third, then add the stock.

Simmer for one hour.

Preheat the oven to 220°C (425°F, gas mark 7).

Pan-fry the mushrooms for 15 minutes, then add to the beef mixture.

Thicken the liquid using the potato flour mixed with the water.

Cool the mixture for 15–30 minutes before using.

Cut 20 circles from the pastry, using a 5 cm (2 in) cutter, then line the bases of the miniature muffin tins with the pastry.

Fill the casings with the beef mixture.

Use a cow-shaped pastry cutter to cut out 20 shapes from the pastry, then place these on top, as lids.

Glaze the tops with egg yolk and bake the pies in the oven for 15–20 minutes, or until golden brown on top.

Chef's Tip

The mushrooms will maintain the intense flavour of the burgundy if added after the beef has been cooked.

Beef and burgundy pies

Makes 20

20	chat (baby) potatoes
	vegetable oil, for coating
	salt and freshly ground black pepper
4	rashers bacon
½ cup	chopped chives
⅔ cup	sour cream

Preheat the oven to 220ºC (425ºF, gas mark 7).

Remove the centre of each potato with a melon-baller and discard.

Rub the potatoes shells with oil and season with salt and pepper.

Bake in the oven for 20 minutes or until roasted.

Dice the bacon finely, then cook in the oven until crisp.

Drain the fat from the bacon and leave to cool for 15 minutes.

Combine the chives, sour cream and bacon in a bowl.

Fill the cavity of the potatoes with the sour cream mixture and bake for a further 10 minutes.

Serve hot.

Chef's Tip

The sour cream mixture can be prepared up to a week in advance.

You can also prepare the potatoes the day before serving, as long as you oil the insides well.

Potato skins with bacon, sour cream and chives

Serves 20

> 5 lamb racks, 4 cutlets on each
> ⅓ cup plain (all-purpose) flour
> 2 eggs, beaten with salt and
>   freshly ground black pepper
> 2 cups Provençal Crumbs (see Master Recipe)
>   salt and freshly ground black pepper
> ¼ cup canola or other vegetable oil

Trim the lamb racks of all fat and sinew.

Separate the individual cutlets.

Take three concave dishes: in the first place the flour, in the second the beaten eggs, and in the third the Provençal crumbs.

Dip the cutlets into each, thoroughly coating with the flour, then the egg and finishing with the crumbs.

Pan-fry in batches using a little of the oil at a time until the cutlets are evenly brown on both sides and the meat just firm to the touch, meaning that it will be pink inside.

Transfer each fried cutlet to a warm (120°C/250°F/gas mark ½) oven until all the cutlets are ready.

Serve hot.

Chef's Tip

> It's much faster to trim the fat and sinew from the cutlets as a rack, then slice them individually, rather than trim each one separately.
>
> Clean the pan of crumbs after frying each batch of cutlets as the residual crumbs will burn, marring the flavour and presentation.

Lamb cutlets with Provençal crumbs

Makes 20

750 g (1 lb 8 oz) fresh hokkien noodles
2 omelettes, each made with 2 eggs
¼ cup oil
10 cloves garlic, finely chopped
1 tbsp salted black beans
(available from Asian food stores)
300 g (9½ oz) Chinese barbecued pork (char siew)
¼ cup chicken stock
3 cups fresh bean sprouts
⅔ cup dried prawns (shrimp)
¼ cup chopped green onion (spring onion or scallion)
¼ cup coriander (cilantro) leaves
1 large red chilli, seeds removed, finely chopped

Singapore barbecued pork noodles boxes

Rinse the hokkien noodles in boiling water, then set aside to drain.

Roll the omelettes and cut into thin strips.

Heat a large wok, pour in the oil and fry the garlic until golden. Set aside to sprinkle on top later.

Add the beans to the wok and stir-fry for 1 minute.

Add the pork and stir-fry for 1 minute.

Pour in the stock and cook for a further minute on high heat.

Toss in the bean sprouts and dried prawns.

Add the noodles and continue tossing until heated through.

Remove from the heat and stir through the spring onions, coriander, chilli, omelette slices and fried garlic.

Serve in New York-style take-out boxes with wooden chopsticks to save on the clean-up.

Master recipes

Béchamel sauce

Makes 2 cups

- 2 tbsp butter
- 2 tbsp plain (all-purpose) white flour
- 2 cups milk
- 2 bay leaves
  salt and freshly ground black pepper

Melt the butter in a saucepan until foaming, then stir in the flour until a thick paste is formed.

Heat the milk with the bay leaves, then pour into the flour and butter mixture, whisking vigorously to prevent lumps from forming.

Simmer gently, stirring all the while, until sauce is thickened and no flavour of raw flour can be tasted. Remove the bay leaves.

Season to taste.

Leek Béchamel

Finely chop the white part of 1 leek. Sauté in the butter until opaque, then add the flour and continue as above.

Potato galettes

Makes 20

- 8 chat (baby) potatoes,
  thinly sliced on a Chinese mandoline slicer
  (it's important that the potato is cut to transparent thickness or it will not mould)
- 1 tsp Maldon (kosher) sea salt
- 2 tbsp virgin olive oil

Mix all the ingredients together.

Press a stack of 6–8 slices firmly into 20 small tartlet cases, creating small, shallow moulds.

Bake in a hot oven until the edges are golden brown and the starch from the potatoes is released to stick the layers together, about 15 minutes

Remove the potato galettes carefully from the tartlet cases to avoid tearing the layers apart.

Chef's Tip

The galettes can be served hot or cold. If you are serving them cold, however, you may want to crispen them in the oven 30 minutes before serving.

Bouillon

Makes 4 cups (1 L)

4 cups	water
1 tbsp	salt
1 tbsp	coriander seeds
1 tbsp	fennel seeds
1 tbsp	mustard seeds
4	bay leaves
1 cup	dry white wine

In a large pot, bring the water, salt, herbs, spices and wine to the boil, then turn down to a simmer.
Add the seafood specified in the recipe, completely immersing it in the liquid.
Simmer for 2 minutes or until the colour changes (prawns/shrimps) or the shells open (clams/mussels).

Chilli jam

Makes 1 cup

2 cups	caster (superfine) sugar
2 cups	large red chillies, seeded and sliced finely on a Chinese mandoline slicer
⅓ cup	lemon juice
⅓ cup	fresh young ginger, finely chopped
1 tbsp	Thai fish sauce (vegetarian, optional)

Combine the sugar, chillies, lemon juice and ginger in a saucepan.
Simmer until the sugar dissolves, stirring occasionally to ensure mixture is not burning at the base.
Increase the heat to reduce the liquid to a syrupy, bright red consistency.
Season with Thai fish sauce and remove from heat.
Cool and store in an airtight container in the refrigerator.

Chef's Tip

Chilli jam keeps for up to 6 months in an airtight container in the refrigerator.
The larger the chilli, the less heat, so for a jam which has kick but is still very palatable use long red chillies.

Green mango salsa

Makes 1 cup

½ medium-sized green mango
  juice of 1½ limes
2 tsp palm sugar (available from Asian food stores)
2 tbsp Thai fish sauce
2 green chillies, seeds removed, cut into narrow rings
1 small fresh kaffir lime leaf, stem discarded, finely shredded
1½ stalks lemongrass, trimmed and finely sliced
2 red eschalots (shallots or pickling onions), peeled and finely sliced
¼ cup mint leaves, finely chopped

Cut the mango flesh from around the seed, then slice into ½ cm (¼ in) cubes.
Mix together the palm sugar and fish sauce until the sugar dissolves, and pour over the green mango 30 minutes before serving. To serve, mix all the ingredients together.

Chef's Tip
Prepare all the ingredients up to a day ahead and store separately in airtight containers.

Hollandaise sauce

Makes 1½ cups

2 tbsp lemon juice
½ cup dry white wine
2 bay leaves
3 egg yolks
1 cup melted butter

Place the juice, wine and bay leaves in saucepan.
Bring to the boil, then simmer to reduce by half to intensify the flavour. Remove from the heat, strain, and allow to cool.
Combine the reduced mixture with egg yolks in a bowl over boiling water.
Whisk constantly over the heat until it develops into a thick, silken consistency. Make sure you move the bowl around so the yolks do not set.
Pour the butter in very slowly, whisking constantly until a creamy consistency is obtained.
Season to taste. If the consistency is too thick, add more lemon juice.

Lime leaf chicken

Makes 1 cup

250 g	(8 oz) minced (ground) chicken
2 tbsp	lime juice
2 tbsp	peanut oil
2	kaffir lime leaves, 1 left whole, 1 finely julienned
1	chilli, seeded and finely chopped
½ cup	finely sliced green onion (spring onion or scallion)
¼ cup	chopped fresh mint
1 tbsp	Thai fish sauce

Cook the chicken in half the juice and oil with the whole lime leaf until the mince loses its translucency.
Stir until the chicken separates like breadcrumbs. Allow to cool.
Once cool, stir in the remainder of the ingredients.
Season to taste; it should be slightly astringent.
Spoon the mixture into your casing of choice, such as a pumpkin square or noodle tart.

Chef's Tip

I suggest using a medium-sized Chinese or Japanese vegetable cleaver instead of a knife. They are excellent for the precise slicing and dicing required in Asian cooking.

Marinated vegetables

Makes 2 cups

All vegetables should be finely julienned.

8	snow peas (mange tout)
1	medium-sized yellow zucchini (courgette)
1	medium-sized green zucchini (courgette)
1	medium-sized carrot
1	medium-sized red capsicum (pepper)
1	medium-sized yellow capsicum (pepper)
2 tbsp	mirin (sweet Japanese rice vinegar)
1 tbsp	Thai fish sauce (vegetarian, optional)

Marinate all the vegetables in the mirin and fish sauce for at least 15 minutes before using. The acid in the mirin cooks the vegetables.

Chef's Tip

The use of the Chinese mandoline to slice and the Chinese cleaver to julienne will greatly assist in this precision work.

Peanut paste

Makes 1 cup

  1 cup freshly roasted peanuts
  1 tsp kecap manis (Indonesian sweet soy sauce)
2 tbsp Chilli Jam (see Master Recipe)
1 tbsp sweet chilli sauce

Place all the ingredients in food processor.
Blend using the pulse button so as not to over-process.
The mixture should bind together well but the peanuts
should be crumb size, rather than ground to a smooth paste.
It should still have crunch and the mixture should hold firmly.

Chef's Tip

    It's great to have some of this paste in the refrigerator to
    crumble through an Asian chicken salad. It can also be
    made with roast cashews.

Mayonnaise

Makes 3 cups

      2 whole eggs
 1 tbsp Dijon mustard
  1 tsp sugar
 ½ tsp salt
 ¼ tsp white pepper
2 tbsp lemon juice
1 tbsp balsamic vinegar
2 cups vegetable oil

Place all ingredients but only one-third of the vegetable oil in
a blender and emulsify.
With the motor running, slowly drizzle in the rest of the oil
until the mixture thickens.

Variations:

Lemon mayonnaise

Add the zest of 1 lemon to the other mayonnaise ingredients.

Tonnato

Use ⅓ cup less oil and add the zest of ½ lemon, 15 capers
and 1 medium-sized can of tuna packed in oil. After the
mayonnaise has thickened, add these ingredients and
process.

Crispy leek

Makes 1 cup

½ leek
1 cup canola or other vegetable oil

Cut the leek into 4 cm (1½ in) lengths.
Slice these in half lengthwise and finely julienne the layers.
Place on a tray of absorbent paper.
Heat the oil on high, then turn down to medium.
Deep-fry the leek until crisp and the colour slightly golden on the edges.
Scoop out and drain on the absorbent paper.
Use immediately or cool and store in an airtight container.

Lemon pistou

Makes 1 cup

2 cloves garlic
¼ cup lemon thyme leaves
zest of 1 lemon
4 tbsp olive oil
½ cup basil leaves
¼ cup pine nuts, dry-roasted
salt and freshly ground black pepper

In a food processor, blend the garlic, lemon thyme and lemon zest.
Add 2 tablespoons of the oil, then blend again.
Combine the basil leaves and pine nuts in the processor and blend again.
With the motor running, slowly pour in the rest of the oil.
Season to taste.

Chef's Tip

Heat the oil gently before you pour it over the herbs. Their colour and flavour will intensify.

Brioche croûte

Makes 20

    5   slices of brioche loaf,
        cut into ½ cm (¼ in) thick pieces
        (day old or frozen is best)
2 tbsp   melted butter

Preheat the oven to 200ºC (400ºF, gas mark 6).
Cut 4 even, 3 cm (1 in) squares from each slice of bread,
discarding the crusts. Use more slices if your bread is not
high enough to provide 4 squares.
Brush with the melted butter, then place on a baking tray.
Bake in the oven for 5 minutes or until golden and crisp to
the touch.
Cool and store in an airtight container.

Chef's Tip

> Freeze the rest of the brioche loaf to make further
> croûtes. It will keep for up to two weeks.

Salsa verde

Makes 1½ cups

    ¼ cup   basil leaves, tightly packed
    1 cup   flat-leaf (Italian) parsley leaves
        1   clove garlic
        3   anchovy fillets
            juice and rind of ½ lemon
       10   sweet gherkins (or cornichons)
   3 tbsp   capers
    1 cup   olive oil
            salt and freshly ground black pepper

Rinse the basil and parsley and dry thoroughly.
With the food processor running, drop in the garlic clove and
chop finely.
Add the herbs then continue adding the rest of the
ingredients, leaving the olive oil until last.
Season with salt and pepper.

Chef's Tip

> Make sure the blade on your food processor is sharp, or it
> will bruise the leaves as it cuts and they will lose colour.
> To store, the salsa verde mixture must be covered by at
> least 2 mm (⅛ in) oil to prevent it discolouring and to
> preserve it.

Shortcrust pastry

Makes 500 g (1 lb)

2 cups plain (all-purpose) flour
1 cup cornflour (cornstarch)
1 cup chopped butter
2 eggs

Sift the dry ingredients into a mixing bowl, making a well in the centre.
Place the butter, then the eggs, in the well.
Work the dry ingredients into the wet mixture gradually with your fingers until mixed through.
Add a little water if the mixture appears to be too dry or if the dough is too crumbly. The pastry should feel like silk to the touch, not sticky or dry.
Refrigerate for 30 minutes before using.

Sweet shortcrust pastry

Makes 500 g (1 lb)

1 cup chopped butter
2 eggs
1 cup icing (confectioners') sugar
2 cups plain (all-purpose) flour

Cream the butter and eggs.
Sift together the sugar and flour.
Place the dry ingredients in a mixing bowl, making a well in the centre.
Add the butter and eggs.
Work the dry ingredients into the wet mixture gradually with your fingers until mixed through.
Add a little water if the mixture appears to be too dry. The pastry should feel silky to the touch, not sticky or dry.
Refrigerate for 30 minutes before using.

Chef's Tip

Place a square of cling film flat on the bench, sprinkle with flour, then roll out your pastry. This makes it easy to remove after cutting and it won't stick to the bench.

Sugar-cured trout

1 medium-sized rainbow trout, skinned,
  boned and cut into small slices, each 2 cm (3/4 in)
  long and 1/2 cm (1/4 in) thick
3 tbsp caster (confectioners') sugar
1 tbsp Maldon (kosher) sea salt
1/4 tsp freshly ground pepper
4 sprigs of dill, leaves only, finely chopped

Mix the trout slices with the sugar, salt, pepper and dill.
Marinate for 1 hour, pouring off all the juices that
accumulate during the curing process.

Chef's Tip

The salt and sugar act as a curing agent for the trout. The
mixture can be kept for up to a week in the refrigerator,
provided the liquid is poured off regularly.

Tomato sauce

Makes 2 cups

2 small onions, chopped finely
2 cloves garlic, minced
4 tbsp virgin olive oil
1 chilli, seeds removed, finely diced
1 kg (2 lb) tinned, peeled egg (plum) tomatoes
  salt and freshly ground black pepper
1 tbsp sugar

Sauté the onions and garlic in half the olive oil until opaque.
Add the chilli and cook for a further 2 minutes.
Add the tomatoes and crush into the onions using a potato
masher.
Season with the salt, pepper and sugar, then simmer for 30
minutes.
Stir through the remaining olive oil and serve.

Chef's Tip

It is always handy to have extra tomato sauce in the
freezer for its infinite variety of uses.
Adding the sugar to the tomato takes away the acidity.

Tzatziki

Makes 1½ cups

1	small Lebanese (Persian) cucumber
1	clove garlic, minced
1 cup	Greek country-style yoghurt
1 tbsp	lemon juice
½ cup	mint leaves, finely chopped
	Maldon (kosher) sea salt, to taste

Grate the cucumber and mix with the garlic, yoghurt and lemon juice.

Stir the mint into the yoghurt mixture.

Season with sea salt.

Serve as a dressing or dip.

Chef's Tip

Using Greek or European yoghurt is important as it is creamy and low in acid, and holds the other ingredients well with less water run-off.

Mustard ice cream

Makes 500 ml (16 fl oz)

4 tbsp	good quality Dijon mustard
5	egg yolks
1 cup	pouring (single) cream
1 cup	milk
4	bay leaves

Beat together the mustard and egg yolks until light and fluffy.

Combine the cream, milk and bay leaves in a saucepan.

Bring to the boil. Pour this mixture over the mustard and egg yolks, then return to the saucepan.

Heat slowly until the mixture coats the back of a spoon.

Remove from heat and cool for 30 minutes.

Churn in an ice-cream maker until thickened to a soft ice-cream consistency.

Store in the freezer for up to 3 months and use as required.

Chef's Tip

Refer to your ice-cream maker's instructions, as some brands require the mixture to be partially frozen before churning.

Good quality Dijon mustard is essential for this recipe. The mustard should have a balanced flavour, no bitter after taste, and the vinegar in it should not be overpowering.

Pizza bases

Makes 500 g (1 lb)

3 tsp	dry yeast
½ tsp	sugar
1 cup	warm water
2 cups	plain (all-purpose) flour
3 tbsp	olive oil
½ tsp	salt

Place the yeast and sugar in a bowl and add a little of the warm water. Leave to bubble for 5 minutes.

Add the flour, then stir in the rest of the water and the olive oil and salt.

Mix together the ingredients until you have a silky smooth dough, adding more water and/or flour as needed.

Knead the dough on a floured surface for about 5 minutes until elastic.

Place the dough in a clean bowl, cover with a damp tea towel (kitchen towel) and leave in a warm place for 1½ hours until it has doubled in size.

Knock back the dough and then knead again lightly.

Roll out the pastry to a thickness of ½ cm (¼ in) on floured cling film.

Cut into 20 squares, 3 cm (1¼ in) x 3 cm (1¼ in).

Proceed with the recipe as required.

Chef's Tip

If you want to make the pizza base a day ahead, prepare the master recipe to pre-baking stage on trays, cover with cling wrap and place in the refrigerator. The chilling prevents the yeast from rising further. Bring to room temperature before cooking.

Provençal crumbs

Makes 3 cups

½	French bread stick, sliced into rounds
½ cup	sage leaves
½ cup	lemon thyme leaves
½ cup	parsley leaves
1	sprig rosemary leaves

Preheat the oven to 180°C (350°F, gas mark 4).

Toast the bread in the oven for about 20 minutes or until dry.

Place all ingredients in a food processor and blend until fine crumbs form.

Acknowledgments

No book comes together without support and collaboration. Many thanks to the following people:

Melissa Corbett, from North Carolina, who has been a constant source of inspiration ever since we met while training at the Cordon Bleu in London and subsequently in the businesses we ran together in London. It was Melissa who helped kick-start this project and gave invaluable assistance in compiling the recipes.

My family. Nana was creator of the best and sweetest in 'small' food: she gave me my first cooking lesson when I was four; Mum, on the other hand, did great 'big' food; Dad must rue the day he said, early in married life, 'It's just food', though he has been the best guinea pig ever since. Tessa, Lucy and Emma, my sisters, for their morale-boosting and practical support.

My staff at Simmer Catering: Sandrine Bonython, for her ongoing loyalty as my business manager; Benjamin Wright, my PA, who spent so many hours deciphering my handwriting; Damien Wright, chef extraordinaire.

Lyn Tranter, my agent, and Cathy Perkins, both of ALM, for their knowledge of their craft, attention to detail and hand-holding.

Julie Stanton, Brigitta Doyle, Angus Cameron and the team at Simon & Schuster for their belief in the project and guiding hand throughout.

Yolande Gray, the book's designer, for her innate sense of style.

John McDonald, a wizard with text.

Paul Del Grande, financial ideas-man who also critiqued the recipes.

Belinda Franks, who taught me, 'that'll do, doesn't do'.

James Nicolle of Wine Planet, who guides me on a continuing basis by marrying the beverages to my food.

The props department: David Heimann of Orson & Blake, who has such great taste in contemporary pieces; Shelly of Mud Australia, who provided contemporary ceramics in gorgeous colours; Sarah Muir of Ivory, for her guidance when it came to the classics.

And Louise Lister, who did the photography, deserves her place in the top echelon of her field. Her practical, can-do bravado is matched only by the magic she performs with a camera.

Index